EMERGENCE FROM CHAOS

EMERGENCE FROM CHAOS

by

STUART HOLROYD

LONDON
VICTOR GOLLANCZ LTD
1957

Printed in Great Britain by
The Camelot Press Ltd., London and Southampton

ACKNOWLEDGMENTS

THE AUTHOR THANKS the following for permission to quote from works still in copyright : Messrs. J. M. Dent & Sons for extracts from Dylan Thomas's *Collected Poems*; Mrs. Yeats, Messrs. A. P. Watt & Son and Messrs. Macmillan & Co. for passages from W. B. Yeats's *Autobiographies*, *Essays* and *Collected Poems*; Messrs. Faber & Faber for passages from T. S. Eliot's *Selected Essays* and *Collected Poems*; The Hogarth Press Ltd. for J. B. Leishman's translation of Rilke's *Sonnets to Orpheus* and *Requiem and Other Poems* and the translation of the *Duino Elegies* by J. B. Leishman and Stephen Spender, and also for extracts from Norman Cameron's translation, *Selected Verse Poems of Arthur Rimbaud*; Mr. R. F. C. Hull for passages from his translation of Rilke's *Selected Letters* published by Messrs. Macmillan & Co.; The Harvill Press for passages from Wallace Fowlie's translation of Rimbaud's *Illuminations*; John Lehmann Ltd. for passages from Norman Cameron's translation of Rimbaud's *Une Saison en Enfer*; The Sylvan Press for the lines from Rimbaud's *Les Premières Communions* translated by Ben Belitt; The Vision Press for extracts from Babette Deutsch's translation *Poems from the Book of Hours* by R. M. Rilke; Messrs. Wm. Heinemann Ltd. for passages from Constance Garnett's translation of Dostoevsky's *The Brothers Karamazov*; Messrs. Rupert Hart-Davis Ltd. for extracts from W. B. Yeats's *Letters*; Messrs. Routledge & Kegan Paul for extracts from T. E. Hulme's *Speculations*, C. G. Jung's *Psychological Reflections* and Karl Jaspers' *Man in the Modern Age*. Quotations from Walt Whitman are taken from *Leaves of Grass* and *Complete Prose Works* in the editions published by D. Appleton. Acknowledgments of shorter passages quoted will be found in the Notes at the end of the book.

CONTENTS

FOR
ANNE

INTRODUCTORY

THE MODERN POET'S world is chaotic within and without. The spiritual chaos which prevails everywhere in our time and which manifests itself equally in indifference to religion on the one hand and fanatical embracing of substitute religions on the other, may have had its cause in political and economic conditions, but its effects have been far reaching and have profoundly influenced the mental life of modern man. The poet is always the most sensitive register of contemporary sensibility, and in this book I have tried to show how a number of poets have reacted to the modern predicament, what means they have used, and to what extent they have succeeded in emerging from the chaos into which they were plunged by the accident of their birth.

There is another, non-historical, aspect to the chaos within man which has relevance to this book. Psychologists call it the unconscious, and by that term we may understand the primitive, blind, animal forces which would impel all of us to aimless, violent and self-destructive action were it not for the control imposed by our conscious and discriminating minds. It is in man's endeavour to overcome this chaos within himself that all religion has its origin. There are various degrees of awareness of the chaotic unconscious, and these degrees are related to various types of religious experience. The six poets I deal with are representative of different types of religious experience and their corresponding degrees of awareness.

In its propagandist aspect this book is an attack on humanism and a plea for the rediscovery of a religious standard of values. There are poets and thinkers of recent generations who have indicated the way that must be followed by the man who does not intend to be submerged in the conflict of the blind and impersonal "isms". The task facing the writers of my generation is first of all to maintain the integrity of their inner life in the face of all external circumstances, and secondly, and by extension, to bring about a world in which a Nietzsche would not go mad, a Rimbaud not be silenced and a Hart Crane not be driven to suicide.

PART ONE

PART ONE

CHAPTER ONE

TWO KINDS OF RELIGIOUS EXPERIENCE

RELIGION IS NOT so much man's attempt to know God as his attempt to know himself. The saint's asceticism and the mystic's ecstasy carry each deeper into himself, to the ultimate still centre where man and God are co-existent. All great religious men are profound psychologists, for they are familiar with the inner life and have explored in themselves all its ways and byways. They know that being religious is not a matter of subscribing to a number of beliefs and accepting a code of conduct, but consists rather in a man maintaining his inner life at its highest pitch of intensity while all the irrelevancies of the world external to him conspire to slacken its tension. Essentially religion is an entirely personal and subjective matter, but in his quest for self knowledge man has tended to project outside of himself the inner processes of his unconscious mind in order to comprehend them the more fully. Thus he has created art and the religious dogma. Certain works of art, and dogmas like that of original sin, afford us a deeper understanding of our own unconscious minds than we could ever arrive at by purely discursive means of thought. The question of the truth of a religion or of its dogmas does not arise, for religion is not justified by its truth but by its efficacy. A religion is anything that a man can live by, and in being lived it finds its truth, which, because it is existential, is irrefutable. This book is not concerned with institutional religion, or with the question whether God, Heaven and Hell have any existence independent of the human mind. These are questions for speculative philosophers and theologians to dispute about. It is conceivable that man's inward religious experiences may have their objective correlatives, and that the images which he uses to project his subjective experience may in some way approximate to these. In other words, God and the Devil may, in a sense wholly beyond the grasp of our terrestrial intellects, exist. But that they exist as psychological realities, in the form of forces within our psyche which we believe to be good and evil, is an indisputable fact, and the only one with which we need concern ourselves.

By defining a religion as anything a man can live by we obviously extend the scope of the term far beyond its usual connotation. The point of the definition is that a religion is something which satisfies a man's needs, and as those needs vary from man to man so do the manifestations of religion vary. Man lives his life on two levels: the first, that of animal life, where his actions are motivated by the necessity of fulfilling his biological needs; and the second, the higher level of mental life, where he becomes a discriminating and creative animal, living not only in the present but with an eye turned towards the past and the future. It is on this second level of his existence that man becomes religious in the true sense of the word. The development of his consciousness beyond the blind animal stage brought with it certain metaphysical needs, particularly the need for some explanation of the nature and purpose of the world in general and of his own life in particular. The more developed religions fulfil these metaphysical needs as well as a man's physical and emotional ones. They satisfy the whole man and have bearing upon every department of human activity, and for this reason they are not merely one aspect of life which a man can accept or reject by choice.

One of the most deeply rooted of human needs is the need to transcend the limits of the self and to participate in a life larger and more permanent than our brief mortal existence. All religions, then, are means of self transcendence, and the distinctive feature of religious experience is a sense of enlargement. In *The Prelude* Wordsworth spoke eloquently about these elemental stages of religious experience. He went to the heart of the matter when he wrote of :

"That most noble attribute of man,
    That wish for something loftier, more adorned,
    Than is the common aspect, daily garb,
    Of human life."

This aspiration towards the more-than-human constitutes the fundamental religious impulse. All religion begins with the feeling that the world revealed to us by our senses is not the whole truth and that man as he at first appears to be is not his true self. Man only recognises his own imperfection because there is in him some faculty which is capable of apprehending an ideal. It is this faculty which elevates him above all other forms of life of which we have knowledge. Through it he experiences that sense of mystical identity with all things, that overwhelming sense of the existence of a deep level of his own being, inaccessible to the reasoning intellect, which is both impersonal, because larger than himself, and the seat and origin of his true personality, his essential humanity.

The experience which we have called the religious impulse inevitably affects a man's actions and leads to the religious endeavour. As Leonardo da Vinci wrote in his note book: "The part always has a tendency to unite with its whole in order to escape from its imperfection."[1]* Once he has glimpsed, albeit momentarily, that other level of existence where life seems to become more meaningful, a man bends all his efforts to raise himself up to it. This, he tells himself, is the essential reality which all the selfish activities of his lower existence obscured from his sight. By harmoniously adjusting himself to this other order of reality man believes that he will realise his highest good.

If we say that the religious endeavour is an attempt to establish a relationship between the I and the not-I, we must bear in mind that the not-I has no inevitable ethical attributes. In other words, it doesn't matter whether the ideal towards which a man aspires is good or bad, his aspiration is still a religious activity. Once we start dictating the

* See Notes, pp. 219-222.

qualities which the ideal should possess we move from the realm of psychology into that of ethics. Whenever a man creates or accepts an ideal and seeks to order himself in relation to it, his actions may be considered to be religious. Thus in Franz Kafka's novel *The Castle*, the frustrated attempts of K. to gain admission to the castle, because they involve all his energies and are the centre around which his life is organised, are a comprehensive symbol for the religious endeavour.

We have not yet encountered that most obvious feature of religious experience: the sense of reverence. Primitive man would have confronted the unsuspected powers of his own psyche with awe, with fear or with wonder. But the process of externalising these powers was a natural one and must have happened very soon after man attained self-consciousness. And when it did happen, when the gods began to arrive, the sense of reverence would have been added to those of wonder, awe and fear. The arrival of the gods is a definite stage in the development of the religious consciousness. A man cannot long maintain his sanity while monstrous images stride down the corridors of his imagination. Again, Wordsworth provides an excellent example of what I mean by this. In *The Prelude* he relates the famous incident of how he stole a boat and rowed out into the lake by night and experienced the terrifying sensation that the mountain on the shore "like a living thing" came after him. He continues:

> "after I had seen
> That spectacle, for many days, my brain
> Worked with a dim and undetermined sense
> Of unknown modes of being; o'er my thoughts
> There hung a darkness, call it solitude
> Or blank desertion. No familiar shapes
> Remained, no pleasant images of trees,
> Of sea or sky, no colours of green fields;
> But huge and mighty forms, that do not live
> Like living men, moved slowly through the mind
> By day, and were a trouble to my dreams."

This "dim and undetermined sense of unknown modes of being" has been called by anthropologists the stage of *animatism*. It is the stage which precedes polydaemonism, or the belief in a large number of spirits animating the natural world, and also polytheism, or the belief in a number of gods. Once man had attained the degree of consciousness necessary for him to observe objectively his psyche's capacity for expansion, the conditions were ripe for him to take a further step up the ladder of the religious life. The fact that this capacity of the psyche seemed to be limitless led to a postulation of a super-psyche (Emerson's "Over-Soul") which was believed to be infinite and "within which every man's particular being is contained and made one with all other".[2] Primitive men may have worshipped their gods motivated by fear or gratitude, but in more developed stages of the religious life the superpsyche or god is revered as a symbol of those experiences in which man transcends his corporeal self.

In his book, *Major Trends in Jewish Mysticism*, Gershom Scholem has made a clear distinction between the two main periods in the history of religion. In the first, of which I have already spoken, there is no abyss between man and God, and all things are bound together in that unity "which precedes duality and in fact knows nothing of it." In the second period "Religion's supreme function is to destroy the dream-harmony of Man, Universe and God, to isolate man from the other elements of the dream stage of his mythical and primitive consciousness. For in its classical form, religion signifies the creation of a vast abyss, conceived as absolute, between God the infinite and transcendental Being, and Man, the finite creature."[3] Now the change-over from the one period to the other was attended by a change in man's attitude to life, and both these changes had their psychological causes. The most obvious and most important of these was man's growing awareness of his own imperfection. As his consciousness developed, as depth after depth of his own being revealed itself to his sight, he must have felt with increasing acuteness the widening gap, on the one hand between himself and all other forms of natural life, and on the other between himself and the ideals which his mind was capable of conceiving. During the eight or nine centuries before Christ many of the great religions made their appearance. One thing they had in common and in which they differed from the primitive religions was their emphasis on man's moral life and their concern with problems. One of the most significant revolutions in history was this one in which the centre of religion shifted from the natural to the moral life of man. In this revolution ethical religion did not displace natural religion, but rather absorbed it into itself. Throughout history the two have interpenetrated each other, and in the combination lies the secret of the uniqueness and indispensability of religion. The natural element prevents religion from becoming merely a branch of philosophy and the ethical element relates it to the problems encountered by man in his communal and personal life.

The emergence of ethical religion was a positive development in the history of man's mind, a definite step forward. It can only be explained if we assume that in the course of his mental evolution some superior faculty gradually came into operation, the seat of his moral sense and the origin of his nobler aspirations. Though I regret to have to use it, the only word available to designate this higher faculty is the well-worn and much-abused one, "spirit". In order to inject some life and meaning into the word I propose to attempt a definition of it which will be suitable for the purposes of the present book.

We are now in territory to which Wordsworth could no longer serve as an adequate guide. If we wished, we could invoke his contemporary, William Blake, who was a man who clearly understood the ways of the spirit. Blake declared that it was his task.

"To open the Eternal Worlds, to open the immortal Eyes
   Of Man inwards into the Worlds of Thought, into Eternity
   Ever expanding in the Bosom of God, the Human
      Imagination."[4]

In this declaration there is a boldness and a metaphysical subtlety which is never found in the poetry of a nature-mystic like Wordsworth. When we move from the poetry of Wordsworth to that of Blake, or from the mystical writings of Madame Guyon or the Quietists to those of St. John of the Cross or Jacob Boehme, we move from an atmosphere which is balmy and relaxed to one which is electric and intense. The intensity is caused by the presence of the element I have called spirit. In Blake's three lines it manifests itself mainly in the thought, though in other instances spirit might express itself equally in feeling or in action.

Spirit has much the same relation to the psyche as blood has to the body. It is the dynamic principle in the psyche. From it stem all man's highest aspirations, his creativity, his sense of justice and his passion for truth, his awareness of beauty and his metaphysical propensities. In it also reside those dark forces which primitive man externalised in the form of demons; in it the powers of good and evil, of light and darkness, of Yin and Yang, wage their eternal war. Spirit is inwardness. It is not equal in all men; in some it is latent and in the rest active in various degrees. It is seen at work in all those situations in which man is required to live most intensely. It is, in fact, the quality which makes him capable of self-transcendence. Spirit is perhaps best conceived as a creative force. It is also a rebellious and autonomous force. It is the ladder by which man seeks to ascend to God, and at the same time the power which enables him to rebel against God. Spirit is energy. Spirit is power. It is spirit that enables man to pursue an idea or ideal at the cost of his comfort or material prosperity. It gives him fortitude in the face of suffering, courage in the face of danger, and makes him capable of heroism and self-sacrifice.

Spirit cannot be pinned down with words, and we could multiply phrases *ad infinitum* and still only circle round it. As Berkeley wrote in his *Treatise Concerning the Principles of Human Knowledge*: "Such is the nature of spirit, or that which acts, that it cannot be of itself perceived, *but only by the effects which it produceth.*"[5] The reader's understanding

of spirit depends ultimately on his own experience of it.
No one can really tell him *what* it is, the most one can do
is to indicate it when it is seen in action and say *there* it is.
It is intangible, but it is nevertheless real, for anything that
acts is actual. And the spirit acts in the intensest way
imaginable. It acts through the intellect in the philosopher
and metaphysician, through the will in the man of action,
and through the imagination in the poet and artist. These
three faculties are vehicles for the spirit; it constantly
expresses itself through them, though it is not wholly contained in them. Through the intellect, the will and the
imagination, spirit urges man to his highest achievements.
It is these achievements that distinguish him from the other
animals; they constitute his whole uniqueness and nobility.

I hope this has conveyed to the reader some idea of the
difference between what we may call psychical and spiritual
experience. The important points to remember are that the
psyche is passive, it does not act, but merely responds to
stimuli; spirit, on the other hand, is active, creative,
dynamic. Psychical experience consists mainly in that sense
of enlargement of which I have already spoken. It may be
had by anyone on a Spring morning or in any other propi-
tious circumstances. It stimulates neither the intellect nor
the will and rarely urges the imagination beyond such
sentiments as

> "God's in his heaven,
> All's right with the world."

(with the inference that as long as God stays in his heaven
the world will get along very well by itself). Spiritual experience is an inner struggle, a tension, a restlessness, an
aspiring towards higher things, an urging forward of the
mind. External circumstances can only precipitate such an
experience, they cannot be its cause. To many people experience of this kind is quite foreign, to others it is the very
stuff of life. Francis W. Newman in *The Soul: Its Sorrows
and Its Aspirations* (1852), distinguishes clearly between the

two types. He writes of the *once-born* and *the twice born*. *The once-born* correspond to those people whose religious experiences are of a purely psychical nature. Of them he says :

"They see God, not as a strict Judge, not as a Glorious Potentate ; but as the animating Spirit of a beautiful harmonious world, Beneficent and Kind, Merciful as well as Pure. *The same characters generally have no metaphysical tendencies: they do not look back into themselves.* Hence they are not distressed by their own imperfections : yet it would be absurd to call them self-righteous ; for they hardly think of themselves *at all*. This childlike quality of their nature makes the opening of religion very happy to them : for they no more shrink from God, than a child from an emperor, before whom the parent trembles : in fact, they have no vivid conception of *any* of the qualities in which the severer Majesty of God consists. He is to them the impersonation of Kindness and Beauty. They read his character, not in the disordered world of man, but in romantic and harmonious nature. Of human sin they know perhaps little in their own hearts and not very much in the world ; and human suffering does but melt them to tenderness. Thus, when they approach God, no inward disturbance ensues : and without being as yet spiritual, they have a certain complacency and perhaps romantic sense of excitement in their simple worship."[6]

There could be no better description of the psychical man, the type of man whom all of us know and most of us are. For this *once-born* type, religion is something he can put on one side as one aspect—he may even admit it to be an important aspect—of life. He enjoys his religious experiences of the psychical kind, but they are of secondary importance compared with his business or family life. The great difference between psychical and spiritual experience is that the latter does not enhance one's enjoyment of life, but rather transforms life completely. The biographies of great religious men are full of experiences—Christ's baptism and subsequent period in the wilderness, St. Paul's vision on the road to Damascus, St. Francis's audition in the church of S. Damiano in Assisi, Jacob Boehme's experience in the fields outside Görlitz and the poet Rilke's in the garden of the Castle Duino—which prove to be decisive points in the man's life; experiences which shift the course of the stream of his life, often in a direction quite contrary to his previous tendencies.

Blaise Pascal had a spiritual experience of the intensest kind and tried to capture something of it in words. His "memorial", which he carried sewn in the lining of his coat and which a servant discovered soon after his death, consists of a series of crude phrases, short exclamations, words almost incoherent but nevertheless expressive of the great amazement and delight which his vision of reality inspired. These words, cast down roughly and artlessly as a personal reminder of a period of transcendental insight, are one of the most vivid descriptions of a spiritual experience in existence. It is worth while quoting them in full.

"L'an de grâce 1654,

Lundi, 23 novembre, jour de saint Clément, pape et martyr, et autres au martyrologe.

Veille de saint Chrysogone, martyr, et autres.

Depuis environ dix heures et demie du soir jusques environ minuit et demi.

Feu.

'Dieu d'Abraham, Dieu d'Isaac, Dieu de Jacob, non des philosophes et des savants.'

Certitude, Certitude, Sentiment, Joie, Paix.

Dieu de Jésus-Christ.

Deum meum et deum vestrum.

'Ton Dieu sera mon Dieu.'

Oubli du monde et de tout, hormis Dieu.

Il ne se trouve que par les voies enseignées dans l'Évangile.

Grandeur de l'âme humaine.

'Père juste, le monde ne t'a pas connu, mais je t'ai connu.'

Joie, joie, joie, pleurs de joie.

Je m'en suis séparé :

Deliquerunt me fontem aquae vitae.

'Mon Dieu, me quitterez-vous ?'

Que je n'en sois pas séparé éternellement.

'Cette est la vie éternelle, qu'ils te connaissent seul vrai Dieu, et celui que tu as envoyé : Jésus-Christ.'

Jésus-Christ.

Jésus-Christ.

Je m'en suis séparé ; je l'ai fui, renoncé, crucifié.

Que je n'en jamais séparé.

Il ne se conserve que par les voies enseignées dans l'Évangile :

Renonciation totale et douce.

Soumission totale à Jésus-Christ et à mon directeur.

Éternellement en joie pour un jour d'exercice sur la terre.

Non obliviscar sermones tuos. Amen."

"The year of our Lord 1654.

Monday, 23rd November, the day of St. Clement, pope and martyr, and of others in the martyrology.

Eve of St. Chrysogone, martyr, and others.

From about half-past ten until about half-past midnight.

Fire

'God of Abraham, God of Isaac, God of Jacob, not of the philosophers and scholars.'

Certainty, Certainty, Sensation, Joy, Peace.

God of Jesus Christ.

My God and your God

'Your God will be my God.'

To forget the world and everything, except God.

He is found only by the ways taught in the Gospel.

Greatness of the human soul.

'Righteous Father, the world has not known you, but I have known you.'

Joy, joy, joy, tears of joy.

I have cut myself off from Him :

The springs of the water of my life have failed

'My God, will you leave me ?'

Let me not be separated from Him for ever.

'This is eternal life : that they acknowledge you to be the one true God, and Him you sent : Jesus Christ.'

Jesus Christ.

Jesus Christ.

I have cut myself off from Him, I have fled Him, renounced Him, crucified Him.

Let me never be separated from Him.

He is held only by the ways taught in the Gospel :

Complete and calm renunciation.

Complete submission to Jesus Christ and to my father confessor.

Eternally joyful for one day of work on earth.

I shall not forget your teachings. Amen."

In all the voluminous literature of religious conversion there are few things more moving than this simple memorial. The exquisite French stylist of the *Pensèes* and the *Lettres Provinciales* is here reduced to being about as coherent as a five-year-old child trying to tell of the wonders it has seen at the zoo. The eminent philosopher and scholar here rejects philosophy and scholarship in favour of the God of Abraham, Isaac and Jacob. The prosperous and distinguished man of the world suddenly sees the vanity of all worldly things, all things, in fact, except God. Reviewing his past life, he is struck down with remorse at having separated himself from God and from the infinitely more "real" reality that he now perceives. He wants the vision, the sense of personality unity with the ultimately real, to last eternally. The only way of effecting this, he believes, is through total renunciation, complete submission to Jesus Christ.

This is but one example of the type of experience I call

spiritual; though other experiences have different causes and are expressed in different terms, they lead always to the same metaphysical conclusions: there is a higher reality than the obvious, tangible, worldly reality, and man is most nearly himself, lives most intensely, when he seeks to embody or to exist upon this higher level. Spiritual experience thus leads to a severe shaking of the foundations upon which the lives of most of us are built. The veils of order and rationality are torn aside and the anarchic, tumultuous, irrational depths of human character and human life stand revealed. The ground which hitherto felt so solid is swept from beneath a man's feet, and the political and social world, the world of petty desires and trade devoted to their satisfaction, becomes unimportant and therefore unreal.

Certain effects follow from this. If the man is to remain sane he must find some new foundations upon which to base his life. Occasionally he may find them in some orthodox religion, but more often than not, in the West at any rate, he sees the Churches as a part of the corruption and falsehood of the life from which he wants to escape. If he has any artistic talent he may reconstruct his vision of the more real world in language, sound, or colour and form. Otherwise he may be driven to some extreme action, to complete renunciation of and retirement from the world, to self-sacrifice for some cause, even to murder or suicide. "Human kind cannot bear very much reality" says T. S. Eliot in the *Four Quartets*; and it is true that once man has been initiated into a vision of reality he must either order his life around that vision, making it supply new foundations to replace the ones it has destroyed, or seek again the security of the world of appearances, or be content to allow the torch of his life to blaze brightly and divinely for a brief hour and then be completely extinguished.

A spiritual experience like Blaise Pascal's may be regarded as the second birth which Francis Newman's *twice-born* type must undergo. Such experiences often have drastic consequences. Invariably they alienate a man from his fellows and make him feel like a rebel within the social order which he repudiates. But nevertheless we cannot ignore the truths that they teach. They point to a higher potential level of human existence, demand the reorientation of human life, the establishment of new foundations. We neglect their message at our own cost.

CHAPTER TWO

SINNER, SAINT AND MYSTIC

THE SPIRITUAL LIFE is a high-level life, and those who live it are the unacknowledged aristocracy of the earth. It is they who make the history in which others are but pawns. They give us our religions and serve as the examples which inspire our highest accomplishments. They are the great solitaries, the most terribly free of men ; and because of this they put on beauty in their lives and in their deaths wear the crown of tragedy. The spirit works through many different kinds of men in many diverse situations, and the study of its various manifestations is one of the most rewarding that a man could undertake. In this chapter I propose to say something about three types of spiritual man, the sinner, the saint and the mystic. We shall encounter these three again in the second part of this book, and it is important that the words should shed their usual vagueness and convey to the reader a definite meaning. So for the moment let us abandon the healthy-minded, psychical man, and see whether a study of the extremes of human degradation and exaltation might not tell us more about man's essential nature and also about those eternal questions to which philosophy and religion continually seek solutions.

Does sin consist simply in the transgression of certain ethical principles, such as those laid down in the Ten Commandments? If so, then we must assume that the man who kills in a moment of anger, the woman who deserts her husband for another man, the liar, the pickpocket, are all sinners. This is the popular opinion, but I would like to diverge from it in order to restore to the word "sin" something of its old religious connotation. The transgression of laws is not sin, it is crime, and is a social problem. The deliberate doing of evil, the conscious siding with the powers of darkness, is genuine sin and is a religious problem. "All manner of sin and wickedness do not make us wicked, so long as they are outside of us,"[1] writes the author of the *Theologia Germanica*, and the fact is that most of the criminals we hear of today are innocent as babes (in the religious, not the social, sense), for the cause of their crime does not lie within themselves, but outside, in their environment, their education or the circumstances of their lives. Such criminals as Hollywood never tires of holding up for our admiration or censure rarely possess intellect, will or imagination to any considerable degree, and are among the most pathetic specimens of mankind. A real sinner, in whom evil is indigenous, is as rare as the coelacanth.

St. Paul would have us believe that sin is weakness. This suggests that the sinner, recognising good as the ideal towards which he should strive, is irresistibly drawn towards evil. This is true only of those petty sins which are better described as transgressions. The fact is that the genuine sinner embraces evil *by his own free choice*, as a way of asserting his independence. In this he shows himself to be, not weaker, but infinitely more strong-willed, than the normal man.

In the fact that man is capable of making a free choice between good and evil lies the whole explanation of what we mean by sin. Nothing may be said to really exist until we are conscious of the existence of its opposite. Good does not exist without the apprehension of evil, nor evil without good. Thus the animal that tears its prey apart, because it is unconscious of the distinction between good and evil, is quite sinless. Man, however, is aware of this distinction, and it is this awareness that gives him the terrible freedom which is the singular condition of human, as distinct from animal, life. At certain times in his life every man comes to a crossroads where he is perfectly free to make an independent choice between good and evil. If he chooses evil the very fact that he was aware of the alternative means that he must carry with him the image of good which will make his evil a reality to him.

This is simply an elaboration of the Christian doctrine of original sin. It is what Dostoevsky's Ivan Karamazov meant when he said, "I cannot understand why the world is arranged as it is. Men are themselves to blame, I suppose; they were given paradise, they wanted freedom, and stole fire from heaven, though they knew they would become unhappy."[2] Dostoevsky understood the psychology of the sinner as well as any man who has ever lived. In his early novel, *Notes From Underground*, we find in complete though undeveloped form the ideas which were to move the destinies of Raskolnikov, Stavrogin and the Karamazov family. The hero of this early novel says:

"One's own free, unfettered choice, one's own caprice, however wild it may be, one's own fancy worked up at times to frenzy—is that very *most advantageous advantage* which we have overlooked, which comes under no classification and against which all systems and theories are continually being smashed to atoms. And how do these wiseacres know that man wants a normal, a virtuous choice? What has made them conceive that man must want a rationally advantageous choice? What man wants is simply *independent* choice, whatever that independence may cost him and wherever it may lead."[3]

It is easy to see how this attitude could lead to crime, especially in the case of the type of man who feels himself to be outside society. For such a man what better way could there be of asserting his freedom than by defying the law? Thus his action would be both a crime in the social sense, and, because it was a deliberately chosen course of action, a sin in the religious sense. Dostoevsky studied such a case in his novel *Crime and Punishment*. Raskolnikov's murder of the old woman in that novel was a cold, deliberate and calculated act, proceeding from the mind of a man who was religious in the most essential sense of the word, for he conceived the purpose of life to be self-transcendence. In order to perform the definitive act that he had decided upon,

Raskolnikov had to strain his will to its utmost pitch of intensity, had to exclude all other things from his mind and centre all his energies upon the one act by which he would assert his independence and raise himself above the level of the generality of mankind.

In *The Possessed* Dostoevsky wrote a study of another extremely interesting type of sinner. When the human intellect has developed beyond a certain point it becomes deeply pessimistic and declares with the Preacher in *Ecclesiastes* that "All is vanity". A man in this state of mind becomes indifferent to everything, to death as well as to life, and can murder with impunity. He may, like Stavrogin in this novel (see particularly *Starrogin's Confession*, Hogarth Press, 1922), commit a series of increasingly atrocious crimes, urged on by a desire to discover if there exists a point where his indifference would give way, where he would become conscious of having sinned. This aspiring towards damnation is essentially the same as the normal man's aspiring towards salvation, and, because it involves the intense exercise of the faculties of will and intellect, is a religious endeavour.

To summarise: there are several senses in which the sinner may be said to be a religious man. He may be so because of the motives which drive him to sin, or by reason of the fervour with which he embraces sin, making it the very centre of his life so that it becomes a kind of substitute religion, and pressing all his powers of will, intellect and imagination into its service.

Of the motives that drive a man to sin it is those that are intellectual, or rather metaphysical, that distinguish him as a spiritual man. That awareness of the insecure foundations upon which everything is built, which, as we saw in the last chapter, is often the result of spiritual experience, may easily drive a man to dissipation or cause him to question the fundamentals of ethics and come to Ivan Karamazov's conclusion that "everything is lawful". Such a conclusion leads naturally into any kind of crime. Or he may sin in order to assert his independence. Man's instinct for freedom is one of his highest aspirations, it is a truly spiritual quality because it is a desire to move beyond the merely animal stage of his consciousness. But the really important point about sin is that it consists in a consciousness of having sided with evil. That consciousness would not be possible without the awareness of the existence of an Absolute Good. Thus, paradoxically, sin "gives God glory". This is perhaps more clearly expressed in Christian terms by saying that it is not those who blaspheme against God and deliberately transgress his laws that are the enemies of religion, but rather those of feeble spirituality who feel they can live comfortably without either God or his laws.

It may be clear to the reader now that the sinner and the saint are not, as most people imagine, poles apart. They are not mortal enemies, though they have a common enemy in all that smacks of mediocrity, in all those who are feeble of will, intellect and imagination. The religious life begins with commitment. Most of us are a complex of various inclinations and emotions, no one of which is strong enough to take precedence over the rest for more than a few hours together. Our energies are used up by a succession of different passions which in turn occupy the centre of our lives. The religious man is he who is capable of committing himself, of enthroning one passion above the rest and making it the centre around which his life revolves. It is not the man who says his prayers and observes the Ten Commandments whom we may justifiably call religious, but rather the man of strong passions, who alone is capable of the renunciation and astringency that a life devoted to an ideal entails. Thus it is by reason of their *absolute dedication* to an ideal that the sinner and the saint are close brothers. Whether that ideal be good or evil does not matter. (Indeed, how are we, with our "Euclidean" intellects, to judge of such a matter? We can only conceive of the Good as it relates to ourselves. And Nietzsche's conception of power as the supreme Good is as valid as any more popularly acceptable ideal). Pagan religions like the Dionysian cults were, in the Christian sense, wholly sinful; yet they were true religions, for their activities involved the whole man

B

and demanded of him intense, undivided and dedicated participation.

The fact is that the saint is just one rung further up the ladder than certain types of sinner. All things, as Heraclitus discovered, tend to turn into their opposites. And in religious conversion, when the centre of consciousness is shifted from one set of ideas, aims and values, to another set, such an upheaval is effected in the individual that all his dearest convictions and most deep-rooted qualities may easily become converted into their direct opposites. St. Paul is of course the classic example of this, and Ivan Karamazov is on the brink of such a complete reversal at the end of Dostoevsky's last novel. The sinner unconsciously strives to be what the saint is. The saint has resolved the conflict between the disparate elements in his personality, has attained wholeness, oneness, by orientating himself towards the Divine principle. In the last analysis he is distinguished from the sinner only by his capacity for the final act of commitment—the act of faith.

It is difficult to draw a composite picture of the saint which is not a meaningless abstraction. We can only say that the distinctive characteristic of all saintliness is a voluntary and complete self-surrender to a Supreme Power. The monk's vows of poverty, chastity and obedience symbolise this complete surrender. By the first vow he sacrifices all his material possessions, by the second he gives up his body, and by the third he makes the most difficult of all sacrifices, that of his will and his intellect.

I believe there is such a thing as a vocational saint, that some men are psychologically so constituted that the way of saintliness, followed by others with such strenuous and self-tormenting effort, appears to them as an inviting and easy road towards which their footsteps are naturally inclined. These men are saints by vocation, for they have little inclination to behave like normal human beings. They are like the hero in Kafka's story *The Fasting Showman*, the Hunger Artist who starved himself simply because his palate was so refined that he could find no food that he liked. These saints have but little sensuality and for them the austere life demands no renunciations that they would not willingly make. They have a horror of all that is brutal or unrefined. Their sensitivity to any kind of discord is excessive. They have no great love for individual people ; nothing, in fact, to tie them to the actual world. Their minds are not the type that continually asks questions, and the idea of the existence of a Supreme Power places little strain on their credulity.

The reader will probably understand from this way Nietzsche felt a great antipathy for the saintly man and considered him to be the most degenerate, weak-spirited and parasitic specimen of the human race. Certainly the vocational saint evinces no sign of possessing intensity of will, intellect or imagination. And in that he is not untypical of other kinds of saint. The act of complete self-surrender, involving the surrender of the right to independent thought, can obviously result in the sapping of a man's intellectual vitality. In becoming a saint a man usually has to exercise his higher faculties, but when he has arrived at his destination of sainthood he often allows those faculties to lapse into desuetude. He no longer needs his will, for there remains nothing for him to overcome thereby ; nor does he need his intellect, for the human intellect must humble itself before the inscrutable Divine mysteries ; nor does he need his imagination, for his insight and the rapture of his communion with the Divine are beyond the scope of any merely terrestrial imagination. He tends to become, in fact, like the Ancients in the last play of Shaw's *Back to Methuselah*, wholly preoccupied with the transcendent wisdom into which he has been initiated.

If this were true of all saints the majority of us would probably side with Nietzsche in regarding them as an unhealthy, morbid bunch. In actual fact it is true only for a small number of them, because it is rare for a saint to regard himself as a saint, to be conscious of having "arrived". It is the world that gives him his title, and very often he himself is acutely conscious of how far he falls short of it.

If the world gives the saint his name, the world must have

some very definite ideas about what it means by saintliness. We may learn something from investigating these popular opinions. The qualities which immediately commend themselves as being of a "saintly" nature are humility, tolerance, love of truth and beauty, selflessness, repose, and a certain remoteness and emotional detachment from all persons and things. The saint is always conceived as a man of pre-eminent *goodness* ; he may be severe with himself, but with other men he is sympathetic and tender. This sympathy is partly fellow-feeling—and in that it is no different from the sympathy of the humanitarian—but there is in it also an element derived from a spiritual understanding of the nature of man. He sees a great gap between man as he potentially is and man as he actually is, and if the minimising of his suffering and the improvement of the conditions of his life will enable man to devote attention to the realisation of his higher potentialities, then the saint is willing to spend his energies on the alteration of those conditions. He does not lack human feeling, indeed he is often one of the most sensitive of men, but his apprehension of a level of existence higher than that where pain and pleasure are the ruling criteria makes suffering, particularly his own, of minor significance.

The popular idea of the saint is, like most such ideas, a half-truth. Gentleness and concern with the welfare of his fellow-men are not inevitable qualities of the saintly man. The one thing which distinguishes him from other men is that by living for an absolute ideal he commits himself to a definite way of life. There can be no compromises in the saintly life ; it is a life of rigorous self-discipline. Though saints may vary in all things else they have this in common : they believe that if anything worth-while is to be accomplished in this life it will be accomplished only through discipline. Man is by nature imperfect and only by the deliberate ordering of his life can he transcend his imperfection. The saint opposes himself to the life of instinct, maybe in some cases because of his hypersensitivity, but usually because he believes that it is only by assuming control over

CHAPTER THREE

ART AND RELIGION

IN THE FIRST CHAPTER we discovered that the common feature of all those experiences that we call religious is that they cause a sense of enlargement. This is a hopelessly inadequate definition for our present purpose of tracing the relationship between art and religion, for it would incline us to the conclusion that all art is religious simply because it takes us out of ourselves and puts us in contact with some other aspect of reality. Obviously any definition which admits the paintings of Sir Joshua Reynolds and the ⌐ vels of Charles Dickens into the category of religious art is t⌐ broad to be meaningful.

Religious and secular art are fundamentally d⌐ ⌐rent in their *sense of values*. The values implied in the work of a religious artist are non-material. In its infancy art was closely associated with the religious life of primitive man, but as civilization developed it began to serve other functions. In the last few centuries a vast amount of literature, painting and sculpture has been produced for the sole purpose of assuring man that the concrete world, the solid world of trade and conventional family life, is th⌐ ⌐nly reality he need bother his head about. This so-called art⌐ not enlarge the mind, but narrows it down so that it sees on⌐ ⌐f-truths. Genuine art is not cleverness, any more than hum⌐ ⌐wit or tragedy mere misfortune. It is the highest impulse⌐ ⌐ human mind ; in it the will, the intellect and the imaginati⌐ work together to give form and substance to those rich and rare moments when the Cloud of Unknowing is for a brief while dispersed, and man is vouchsafed a vision of that more constant order of reality of which he is normally but dimly aware. In secular art, however, there is no hint of the existence of any order of reality other than the material. The fact that such art is edifying or contains fine "Christian senti-ments" does not make it religious.

Having eliminated materialistic art from the religious category we are still left with a wide diversity of works. Now the answer to the question, What makes a work of art religious? obviously depends on your interpretation of the word "religious". A religion is any system of thought or any ideal that a man can live by. This is true, but it is tanta-mount to saying that it is any system that fulfills a man's needs, and we are back to the fundamental question, What are the needs that a religion satisfies? Of course, they vary with ages, races and individuals, hence the many different religions that have existed in the world. But common to all are the basic needs for : (1) an explanation of the purpose of life ; (2) some assurance that man is exempt from the observed transience of other forms of natural life ; and (3) an ideal to worship and aspire towards. Insofar as an artist possesses any of these needs his art is inclined to be religious. This does not necessarily mean that in his art he seeks answers to the question of immortality or of the purpose of life, but that all his work originates in a consciousness which is aware of these problems. Art is not religious because it concerns itself with obviously religious subjects, but rather because the artist's attitude to life is a religious one. Cézanne's still-life paintings are genuine religious art, whereas many of the Renaissance pictures of the Madonna and Child and similar subjects are not religious in the strict sense of the word, for the emotions which they express are purely human ones.

At this stage I think we will find it more rewarding to consider art as the expression not so much of religious experience as of a religious attitude. Even when it appears to be spontaneous, a direct response to some experience, as is much lyrical poetry, it is invariably consistent with the poet's attitude to life before and after his experience. So we will get to the root of the question of the relationship between art and religion by studying various common religious attitudes rather than individual experiences.

A man's religious attitude is conditioned by all his experiences, physical and intellectual. It is influenced by his education, his environment, the thought-habits of his age, and by his own psychological constitution. Though these attitudes may vary greatly in small points they lend themselves to classification in two groups, the one optimistic and the other largely pessimistic. The optimistic one I shall refer to as the pseudo-religious attitude, but will first of all say something about the attitude which I believe to be the authentic one.

The religious attitude begins with disillusionment, with the realisation that "all is vanity", that the life to which most people devote all their energy is mere illusion, that man is wretched because he can apprehend a perfection which he is incapable of realising. This dissatisfaction with life as it is develops only in a mind which has a higher concept of human destiny than is common among most people, a mind which has the sincerity to follow its intuitions to their inevitable conclusions and the courage to face those conclusions even though they seem to be negative ones. In this attitude all the great religions had their origin. It is an attitude which, instead of looking down at the lower animals and saying "what a noble creature man is", looks up to the highest ideals conceivable by the human intellect and says "what a miserable and imperfect creature man is". And having realised this the religious man does not, as his critics suggest, just sit down and moan about his condition, but takes positive steps to improve it, to better himself and approach a little nearer to the ideal which his mind is capable of conceiving. There is a certain anti-human element in the religious attitude, for man is subordinated to an absolute set of values. The attitude as I have defined it has no universal ethical implications. There are as many codes of ethical values as there are different ideals. The practice of making human sacrifices, though repugnant to one religious attitude, is quite consistent with another. And this does not imply any fundamental difference between the attitudes, but merely a difference between the ideals which they hold sacred.

Religious values are quite independent of human feelings and desires, they are absolute and objective.[1]

The pseudo-religious attitude measures all things with the yardstick, Man. It perceives no radical imperfection in man and is not troubled with a tendency to reflect upon the vanity of human life. But man's religious needs are deeply rooted in him and are not affected by the rationalism which invariably attends this optimistic view of life. He must have an ideal to look up to and worship, however irrational that may be, and if his surface intelligence forbids him to believe in a non-human Deity he will invent one according to human concepts. Similarly with ethical values, if he cannot subscribe to any absolute code he will invent one which is relative to man, and his values will be derived from the human feelings and desires which they are intended to chasten and control. The result is a situation in which a man is judged according to the standards which he himself dictates. It is a vicious circle from which there is no escape except to the authentic religious attitude with its absolute and incorruptible code of values.

We shall see in a moment how drastic the consequences of this humanistic attitude can be, but before proceeding to this we cannot allow the authentic religious attitude to pass without criticism. Obviously there are potential evils in its anti-humanism. It is easy to see how it may give rise to intolerance, indifference to human life, fanaticism and arrogant dogmatism ; how it did give rise in fact to the *autos-da-fé* of the Inquisition, and, nearer our time, to the horrors of Belsen and Buchenwald. But these are not inevitable consequences of the authentic religious attitude, but rather perversions of it caused by its exalted ideals gripping the imaginations of people who were sadly lacking in intellect.

Living, as we do, at the end of a long period of Humanism, we have a great deal of material to hand for our criticism of this attitude. During the four centuries which have passed since the Renaissance the Humanistic categories have dominated men's thought. In other words such doctrines as that of the perfectibility of man have become, to the minds of most people, not doctrines but irrefutable truths. The consequences of this are seen both in the political and the cultural situation prevailing today. If we confine ourselves to the study of its influence on art the weaknesses of the pseudo-religious attitude will be quite clearly revealed.

Shaw observes in the preface to *Back to Methuselah* that Michael Angelo "could paint the Superman three hundred years before Nietzsche wrote *Also Sprach Zarathustra* and Strauss set it to music."[2] What Shaw does not state is that those three hundred years form a consistent whole, a definite period in the world's history, the period of European Renaissance Humanism. The reason why Michael Angelo and Nietzsche have so much in common is that they shared a way of thinking, an attitude to life, which was common to their period. For the same reason Zarathustra would have approved of Marlowe's Tamburlaine. Nietzsche was a solitary figure in the nineteenth century, upholding the high ideals of his Renaissance ancestors, the ideals which had been corrupted by his contemporaries and immediate predecessors. And while he was singing of the Superman, Tennyson and Swinburne, inheritors of the same tradition, were constructing their anaemic and sentimental verses. Humanism had declined, as was inevitable, into romanticism and bourgeois sentimentality. This was the result of the human and the divine not being completely separated. A fixed and definite ideal, an absolute set of values, keep a man up to the mark. But an ideal conceived in terms of the human is necessarily a projection of man's weaknesses as well as of his moral strength. An ideal which is mobile and able to accommodate itself to the needs of the moment is ineffective as a standard for conduct. Of course the Humanist denies that man is radically imperfect, and therefore does not see that any exalted idea *must* eventually become corrupted. Viewing it historically we can see for a fact that the high ideals of the early Renaissance artists and thinkers rapidly declined into the state of mind prevalent in the early eighteenth century, when man was a "social animal" and nothing else and art was concerned with the trivialities of the external, social life. Had any artist devoted himself to a searching analysis of the inner, spiritual man, he would certainly have been regarded as unfashionable and somewhat improper. Swift, of course, was so regarded, and he was one of the very few men of that age who could be described as religious in the true sense of the word, one of the few who could see lurking behind appearances the elemental chaos of the world. But his savage indignation was quite ineffective, and he comes down to us as an outsider in a period of which the typical artistic products are Pope's ethereal and exquisitely accomplished *Rape of the Lock* and the pretentious portraits of Romney and Kneller.

The pseudo-religion which takes man as its ideal is psychologically ingenuous because it fails to recognise that man is an inconstant and variable creature. There is nothing in Humanism to maintain the human ideal at its highest level. The gap between the human and the divine which is recognised by the authentic religious attitude results in the sense of sin as the gap widens. But for the humanist there is no such gap, and for him a "fall from grace" is impossible, because if he falls his ideal falls with him. Thus the problem of evil disappears from Humanist thought. This is not mere abstract argument, but a truth which has a profound influence on many aspects of life. We are all acquainted with the very human tendency to rationalise and justify to oneself behaviour which one knows to be morally wrong. The Humanist persuades himself that the ethical values which he invents and which are relative to himself are the right ones, whereas the religious man, though he may choose to do wrong, does not persuade himself that he is doing right, and is aware of his sinfulness because he remains subordinate to the absolute values which he acknowledges as right.

There are many different aspects of the human character and it was inevitable that the emphasis should at some time be shifted from the spiritual man, to man, the political animal. This happened with Rousseau. In the celebrated first sentence of *The Social Contract*, "Man is born free but is everywhere in chains", the important words "man" and "free" can have only a political connotation. A pre-Renaissance thinker would have said just the opposite of this and his statement would have contained a profounder truth, for it would be concerned with man's essential self. He would have said: "Man is born in chains and it is his duty and destiny to win for himself a degree of freedom." These two statements may be taken as typical of, and symptomatic of the difference between, the two attitudes we are studying.

The dignity of the human mind and the nobility of its thought are best fostered and protected by the authentic religious attitude. The example of art teaches us that when the Humanistic categories dominate men's minds they encourage a flaccid and sentimental way of thinking. Genuine religious art has a certain hardness, precision and austerity which Humanist art lacks. In painting the religious emotion manifests itself in a tendency towards abstraction and a desire to subdue life in the purely human sense and to dispose of all accidental details. Thus in Byzantine mosaics the human figure is stylised and in the Persian carpet the design is always of an abstract nature. In poetry we can observe a similar tendency. The poet with the genuine religious temperament, no matter what he writes *about*, introduces a certain austerity and conciseness into his work. The romantic poet just gushes out his feeling, believing that feeling itself is the highest virtue in poetry. But the religious poet is wary of human emotion and believes it to be his business not so much to feel as to *shape feeling*. He seeks to sublimate mere feeling and make of it "a poem as cold and passionate as the dawn."[3]

Many of the so-called "metaphysical" poets of the seventeenth century had the authentic religious attitude to life. Mr. Eliot has pointed out that there was a decline of sensibility in the century separating Donne and Gray. The feeling in early eighteenth-century poetry is *cruder* than that in the poetry written a hundred years previously. Compare Thomas Gray's *Elegy in a Country Churchyard* with any typical poem by Donne, Herbert, Traherne, Vaughan, Crashaw, Stanley

or Marvell. To a mind that has managed to free itself from
the Humanist attitude it is a transparently platitudinous and
sententious poem. The poet's sentiments are inflated and
insincere, his use of emotionally-toned words and stilted
phrases quite shameless, and his pedantic and monotonous
stanza form is in no way suited to the subject matter. The
Romantic poets of the early nineteenth century reacted
against the worldliness of their grandfathers, but with the
one exception of Blake they were unable to escape from the
now firmly rooted Humanistic categories of thought. For
them the human and the divine were still confused, hence
the pantheism of Wordsworth's *Intimations of Immortality*
Ode and of Shelley's *Adonais*. To bring the story up to date
we need only observe the relapse which took place during
the Victorian age. The material prosperity of that period
and its completely worldly values caused poetry to be considered as a merely pleasant pursuit, or perhaps as the science
of the pretty-pretty, for everything had to masquerade as a
science in those days if it was to be regarded seriously. As
a consequence of this we get the insufferable sentimentality
of parts of Tennyson and Swinburne, poets whose use of
language is calculated to induce hypnosis and lull to sleep
all man's higher faculties. This was the climax of Humanism,
or rather its very lowest water mark, and we are still a long
way from shaking ourselves free of all its influences. The
ideal of Humanism had shifted from the spiritual man to the
social, political, material man ; now it took a further step and
became the religion of the man-made, the faith in Progress.
In Tennyson's *Locksley Hall* occur these words, the very
limit of Humanistic complacent and optimistic arrogance :

"Not in vain the distance beacons. Forward, forward let us
    range,
  Let the great world spin for ever down the ringing grooves
    of change.
  Thro' the shadow of the globe we sweep into the younger
    day :
  Better fifty years of Europe than a cycle of Cathay."

A similar vision of the great world spinning for ever down the ringing grooves of change would cause the deepest pessimism in a genuine religious man. It would evoke a feeling similar to Pascal's when he cried "the immensity of these infinite spaces frightens me". Inevitably the question had to be asked, What is this limitless change, this so-called Progress, *leading to*? Such questions lead directly to the questioning of the fundamental issues, the premises underlying all Humanist thought. In Part Two of this book we shall see to what extent modern poets have done this.

What has emerged so far, I hope, is that religion in art is not something external, in the subject matter, but something subjective, in the artist's attitude to life. We have considered the two main attitudes and noted how they influence the work of the artist. To summarise them briefly :

A. The authentic religious attitude :
    separates the divine and the human,
    subordinates man to absolute values,
    produces an art which is austere, hard, precise, sometimes static and sometimes tending towards abstraction.
B. The Humanist or pseudo-religious attitude :
    takes Man as the measure of all things,
    has values which are conveniently capable of adjusting themselves to human needs,
    produces an art which may be highly idealistic and dynamic or vague and sentimental, depending on the character of the artist.

Perhaps the reader will understand now what Yeats meant when he said "When I look at the photograph of a picture by Gauguin, which hangs over my breakfast table, the spectacle of tranquil Polynesian girls crowned with lilies gives me, I do not know why, religious ideas".[4] By using the word "tranquil" here, Yeats provided a partial answer to his implied question. Much religious art has this quality of tranquillity, of eternal repose, the fruit of those moments when the artist attains to a kind of union with the divine. It is only the genuine religious artist who apprehends that world of pure Being, of the One, the Perfect, the Absolute, which in the Christian religion is represented by the Blessed Trinity. Ruysbroek describes the dual character of the Absolute as: "Tranquillity according to His Essence, activity according to His Nature: perfect stillness, perfect fecundity".[5] And Eckhart means exactly the same when he distinguishes between God and Godhead: "God acts, the Godhead acts not, it has no act to perform, no action proceeds in it. It has never purposed an act. The distinction between God and Godhead lies in action and non-action".[6] The Humanist naturally denies the world of Being, of the Godhead. Accustomed as he is to thinking in human terms, the idea of perfect stillness, of intense Being, of pure Existence without action, is inconceivable to him. Indeed it is often an idea which is positively distasteful to him. Nietzsche makes Zarathustra say:

"Evil I declare it and hostile to mankind—this doctrine of the One, the Perfect, the Unmoved, the Sufficient, the Intransitory!

"The Intransitory—it is but a simile! And the poets lie exceedingly—

"But the best similes shall speak of Time and Becoming; they shall be for praise and justification of all transitoriness."[7]

But for the mystic and the genuine religious poet the world of Being, "the still point of the turning world" as T. S. Eliot calls it in *Burnt Norton*, is a reality.

The art of the world of Becoming, which gives expression to the struggles involved in the religious life, is the most familiar type of religious art to Western Europeans. Some artists have been convinced that they were vocationally bound to the world of Becoming.* This is not necessarily true, as we shall see if we ask the searching question, What

* Yeats for example. See pp. 130-132.

is it that makes the religious man want to express his experiences in art? There are, I believe, two main answers to
this. First, for one type of artist there is the desire to clarify
his experiences to himself, to work out his destiny through
his art. He feels within himself a confusion of forces and
ideas, urging him in several directions, which, in order to
preserve the balance of his mind, he needs to objectify and
get into focus. Secondly, there is a desire in some artists to
create something beautiful, perfect and permanent, a desire
which is often a reaction against the ugliness, imperfection
and transience of worldly things. These are the two most
common motives underlying religious art. The first tends to
produce the dynamic art of the world of Becoming and the
second the static art of the world of Being. But rarely is one
of these motives found in its pure form, without some admix-
ture of the other, and consequently few works of religious
art can be said to be either wholly dynamic or wholly static.

Behind Humanist art there are often quite different
motives at work. One of the most common of these is the
desire to glorify oneself. Since Humanist art cannot be God-
centred it tends to be self-centred, and the artist values and
cultivates and delights in parading his supposedly individual
personality. Now for the religious man the artist's personality, meaning his idiosyncrasies and the points wherein he
differs from other men, is of no great interest. The artist is
most worth listening to when he transcends the limits of
selfhood. This does not mean that he must become entirely
depersonalised. Like Blake and certain modern poets he may
have an individual vision which he expresses in personal
imagery. The religious artist does not need to suppress his
personality entirely, but simply to purify it and get rid of
everything in it that is trivial and accidental. The new power
which a religious conviction gives causes a transfiguration of
the personality in order to relate it to the new values which
occupy the centre of consciousness.

Of course, self-glorification is not the only motive behind
Humanist art. If it was, the distinction between Humanist

and religious art would be easily made and there would be no difficulty in choosing between the two. In theory the distinction is quite clear, but when we come to study individual artists we invariably find that they have a disconcerting tendency not to conform to our plan. This does not mean that our plan is invalid but that its usefulness is limited. It serves to show us our subject from a distance, to reveal to us the historical pattern and the fundamental similarities and differences between various artists, which a closer view, a detailed study of one artist or period, would tend to obscure. The over-simplification which results from our taking the bird's eye view must be remedied by our coming back to earth and realising that artists cannot be classified like butterflies.

The fact that we had to call the Humanist attitude a pseudo-religious one is evidence enough that the two attitudes cannot be sharply divided. When a man has religious feelings or convictions they occupy the very centre of his consciousness and when he gives expression to them he does so with an intensity which makes you realise that the whole man, not merely his intellect, is involved. A similar intensity of feeling is often found in Romantic poetry. As T. E. Hulme observes, the Romantic poet never tires of "dragging in the infinite". This emotional intensity and feeling for the infinite is enough to persuade most people that Romantic art is religious. And so, in a sense, it is. But in order to avoid confusion we must distinguish between it and the type of religious art which originates in an entirely different attitude towards man and life. Authentic religious art is, first of all, disciplined ; it is not born of a vague sense of the infinite, but of a feeling for a definite ideal towards which the artist aspires and to which he is subjugated.

In conclusion, in order to establish quite clearly the criteria according to which I shall attempt an assessment of the poets dealt with in Part Two, I propose to give an answer to the question : What qualities are required in a religious poet of the first order ? The qualities are, I suggest, a capacity for spiritual suffering, an exalted concept of Deity, a realization of the reality of evil and a consequent view of the world which is not blindly optimistic. I will elaborate each of these points in turn.

Spiritual suffering is that restlessness of the spirit which urges the mind to be ever seeking answers to the eternal questions. There are some men who are psychologically so constituted that the question of the purpose of life *matters* more than anything else to them. They suffer acutely if they cannot find a satisfactory answer to their questions. They cannot always subscribe to the answers provided by the great Faiths, but are driven to seek some answer which will be more compatible with their own intellectual and emotional constitution. They are not unbelievers, at least if it is true that "the unbeliever is, as a rule, not so greatly troubled to explain the world to himself, nor so greatly distressed by its disorder."[8] They are doubters rather, individuals with the will to believe who are incapable of making the intellectual sacrifice that belief entails. It is often exactly the disorder of the world that prevents them from believing. They declare with Ivan Karamazov that "in the final result I don't accept this world of God's, and, although I know it exists, I don't accept it at all. It's not that I don't accept God, you must understand, it's the world created by him that I don't and cannot accept."[9] And like Ivan Karamazov they may be driven to actual physical illness by the intensity of their spiritual suffering. Of course Ivan Karamazov is an extreme example and I am not saying that the great religious poet should be like him, but I do believe that even though he is an orthodox believer he must not be complacent in his faith, must not cease to ask questions or allow the seeds of doubt to die in him. No poet was ever more orthodox than Gerard Manley Hopkins, nevertheless his so-called 'terrible' sonnets testify to the fact that he underwent the the most acute spiritual suffering.

The second essential in a religious poet of the first order is an exalted concept of Deity. Many gods have existed at different times and indeed still exist today, and they have all encouraged poets to sing their praises in the most absolute terms. How are we to choose between the primitive man's harvest god and the God of the Christian? Can we justify our belief that the one is superior to the other? If we consider them in relation to the art they produce, I think we can. The primitive's prayers for favourable weather or hymns of thanksgiving for a good harvest originated from purely selfish motives, from a desire to satisfy the needs of the biological man. For the thinking Christian the idea of a god who is solicitous of our every selfish whim is today insupportable. And Christian art is superior in that it holds not the biological man but the spiritual man to be para-mount. The God of the Christian does not encourage the artist to pursue his own paltry good, but requires him to sacrifice some of his self-interest for the sake of that higher good the attainment of which satisfies his deepest needs. Thus that concept of Deity is the most exalted which sets the highest ideals for man and demands the greatest sacrifice of him.

Now poets are often egregiously self-centred fellows and such a Deity is not always possible for them. In fact we find that very few of the greatest poets subscribe to an orthodox theology. They often have very different ideals, and we must not be deceived by their use of the words God, Devil, Heaven, Hell, Angel and the like, but must ask what these words symbolise for the individual poet. They may mean almost anything, and it will be one of our tasks when we come to study the poets in Part Two to find out what are the ideals which they apprehend as being divine.

Finally I have said that a religious poet must realise the reality of evil and have a consequent *Weltanschauung* which is not blindly optimistic. Optimism shows but one aspect of reality, reveals the world in two dimensions. But I esteem that the greatest poetry which takes account of all the facts of human experience, not excepting the unpleasant ones. The poet who is unaware of evil and not concerned with the problem of sin can at best only apprehend a very small part of the truth. The great artist was always an uncompromising realist, drawing the whole world into himself, the ugly as well as the beautiful, and there seeking to contain it and to relate and reconcile all contraries and dichotomies. The art of the pre-Raphaelites, because it lacked the vision of ugliness, seems to us now a false beauty, a mask which conceals the reality of life. Good and evil, ugliness and beauty, sin and redemption : these antinomies are for ever straining against each other like two teams straining at a rope in a tug o' war. Man is that rope and the greater the contending forces within him the greater will be the creative, spiritual tension. While the forces are equal the rope appears to be still, but beneath the stillness is concealed a concentration of energy. And if one team were suddenly to release its grip on the rope the other would fall down in confusion and the game would be over. Similarly, if the mind relaxes for a moment its awareness of good or evil, ugliness or beauty, sin or redemption, its grasp of reality becomes chaotic and unreliable. And between the optimistic and pessimistic attitudes to life there exists the same essential tension. No mind that is capable of contemplating the world as it is, and the facts of human experience, can avoid a degree of pessimism. But both optimism and pessimism are dead ends for the creative artist, and the one must always be tempered with the other. The greatest artist is he who is deeply aware of the reality of evil, ugliness, sin and suffering, and can yet affirm the world. If he deliberately ignores any aspect of reality he can but create a false beauty.

The congenital optimism of the Humanist attitude has been severely shaken in this twentieth century. The faith in progress is still very strong, but here and there individuals have been waking up and asking, Where is it all leading to? And the answers which the more far-sighted of them have been constrained to give to this question have brought the Devil back into our world with a vengeance. The vision of evil has returned into modern art. And when these negative elements, the vision of evil, disillusionment and the sense of the vanity of life, have been ripened in the solitude of the human heart, there emerges out of them something positive and rejuvenative, namely the authentic religious attitude.

We shall see later that this has happened in the work of several modern poets. M. André Malraux testifies to the fact that there has been a parallel development in the arts of painting and sculpture. In *The Psychology of Art* he writes :

"The history of Italian art in the thirteenth and fourteenth centuries records the gradual retreat of the powers of Evil. For us, those forms of Baroque from which the Jesuits succeeded in eliminating Satan have far less cogency than their Spanish counterparts in which Hell always has a place. . . . The Devil lurks behind all arts of immobility . . . and almost always Satan paints in two dimensions. Most of the works in which we can trace his hand have come back to life today. We seem to hear a furtive colloquy in progress between the statuary of the Royal Portal at Chartres and the great fetishes—in voices differing as vastly as the tone of an indictment meant to save man's soul can differ from one that voices sheer despair. But when an art is groping for its truth, all forms are allies that impugn those arts whose falsity it knows. By contrast with the nineteenth, our century stands for a Renaissance of Destiny."[10]

CHAPTER FOUR

THE RENAISSANCE OF DESTINY

ART, THEN, IS NOT mere diversion, but is tied up with life at every point, and the destiny of the artist is inseparable from that of the world in which he lives and works. In this chapter we shall take a look at the world into the midst of which the modern artist is plunged, try to trace some of its currents of thought and face some of its problems. This is the final setting of the scene. Before bringing on the poets themselves we must provide them with a historical frame consisting of some at least of the events, conditions and ideas which have governed their destinies.

The word which best epitomises the manifold problems of our time is "alienation". A century ago the Danish thinker, Kierkegaard, foresaw that the relentless "levelling process" which man had set in motion by developing his industrial civilisation must inevitably lead to the despiritualisation of man and to "the tyranny of equality". In 1848 he could see clearly what George Orwell saw just a hundred years later when he wrote his *1984*. And Kierkegaard realised then that "the levelling process can only be stopped by the individual attaining in his loneliness the courage and dauntlessness of a religious man answerable to God".[1] But 1848 was also the year of the *Communist Manifesto* of Marx and Engels, and the statements of the lonely and obscure Danish thinker could do nothing to hinder the levelling process which this well-intentioned document accelerated.

1855 was the year of Kierkegaard's death, and it was also the year in which Büchner's *Kraft und Stoff*—the most complete statement of the philosophy of materialism—was published. Four years later, in 1859, Darwin published his *Origin of the Species*. This famous book encouraged the cause and effect view of the world, the mentality that could

not view a gap in nature without reacting violently and bending all its efforts to bridging it. The geologists had already
provided the material for the doctrine of the evolution of the
earth, thus enabling philosophers to dispense with the irrational idea of an act of creation. So towards the end of the
nineteenth century all knowledge, and particularly metaphysical knowledge, was tied up in a compact little parcel
with all the loose ends tucked neatly away, and the conditions
were ripe for Herbert Spencer and other philosophers to
come forward with their mechanical interpretation of human
life and their optimistic faith in Progress.

The foundations of this faith were given a severe jolt by
the First World War. The spiritual chaos which swept over
Europe after it, and of which we can see the expression in
T. S. Eliot's *Waste Land*, had been brewing for some
decades. Several artists—James Joyce is an obvious example
—had built their arks of artistic detachment and were able
to ride secure above the deluge. Their deliberate detachment
from a world that was rushing precipitantly and blindly
towards the edge of the abyss was an act of heroic defiance, a
desperate act, but one which implied no remedy to the situation. The words of T. S. Eliot represent the attitude of all
the serious artists of his generation :

"These fragments I have shored against my ruins."[2]

The use of the word "my" suggests that art had become an
entirely personal affair. Artists no longer believed that they
could redeem mankind or civilisation, it was enough if in the
face of adverse circumstances they could remain true to
themselves and to the values that were meaningful for them.
The artist is by nature and tradition the upholder of spiritual
values, and in an age when material values are predominant
he becomes cut off from the majority of his fellows.

But alienation means more than the solitude of the artist.
It means that the individual is divided within himself, that
there is a barrier between his essential self and his superficial
social self. Men meet and exchange words and put on an act

of good fellowship, but the pretence cannot be kept up for long and when the host sees his last guest depart the smile fades from his face. In the twenties (and the same is true of our time) there was no activity in which men's deeper selves could participate communally. The theatre, despite the efforts of Shaw, O'Neill, Yeats and Synge, was for the most part "escapist", as also was the entertainment provided by the infant art of the cinema. "One thing I did not foresee", Yeats had to admit when he came to write his autobiography, "not having the courage of my own thought: the growing murderousness of the world".[3] Dostoevsky and Kierkegaard had foreseen it and had also seen that the only hope of salvation lay in man's sense of personal responsibility before God. But by now God had become an anachronism, or at least the living God had been usurped by the god of the machine. And this was the most tragic of all forms of alienation.

Rousseau and the Romantics had been aware of man's growing alienation from the natural world. But their "return to nature" doctrine is no panacea for a civilised community. Man does not realise the fullness of his personality by harmonising himself with nature. It is his destiny to be ever moving forward into a higher state of consciousness, and by no exertions can he win from fate a return to the animal condition of innocence. Rousseau and the Romantics were incapable of understanding the true nature of man and the significance of the Christian dogma of the Fall. The alienation they felt was a reality, but it was the alienation of the psyche. Equally real, and doubly pernicious, is the alienation of the spirit, alienation from God.

Many readers will be inclined to interrupt at this point and ask "What exactly do you mean by that?" The question is justified, for today no writer can assume that such phrases as "alienation from God" communicate anything to the vast majority of his readers. In the first chapter we said that man's idea of God is a projection of his own highest aspirations and a symbol of those experiences wherein he transcends his corporeal self. Further, it is in the exercise of his spiritual faculties, his will, intellect and imagination, his passion for truth and justice, his appreciation of beauty, that man approaches nearest to God. Alienation from God means, first of all, the corruption of these faculties. It means that the goal towards which human effort is directed is not the adjustment of the self to a transcendental order of reality, but rather the establishment of a harmonious relationship with the material world, the world of "getting and spending". When man is separated from God he does not become, as the atheist boasts, a "free-thinker". Significant thought can never be free, because it is always conditioned by the mental attitude of the thinker, by certain absolute and ineradicable premises which underlie the thinking even of the most analytical mind. When the "free-thinker" rejects God what he really does is move voluntarily from a large cage into the confines of a smaller one. The range of his possible significant thought becomes limited to social and political issues.

If one word had to be chosen to drive a nation to war or to rouse in a man a passion of righteous indignation the word "freedom" would surely be infallible. The very word seems to set man's blood boiling, and for some vague idea of freedom many millions of men have sacrificed their lives. Today politicians speak of "the free countries of the world" quite seriously, without suspecting that there is a sinister irony in the phrase. Genuine freedom is not possible for a nation or individual that is alienated from God. The external freedom of which the politician speaks, the freedom to conduct your life according to your inclinations, do, say and think what you like, is only partial freedom. More important is the inner freedom of the man who has risen above the prejudices and thought-habits of the majority of his fellow men and is capable of independent thought. When we are externally free we are often blinded to the fact that our inner freedom is limited. In the so-called "free countries of the world" today there are numerous influences at work on the minds of both children and adults which make it impossible for the majority of them to think independently.

Man achieves his highest possible degree of freedom when he stands personally responsible for his actions before God. If he feels responsible only to some political cause or some such secular ideal he will never be inwardly free. For this reason the oppressor is often less free than the oppressed. He sacrificed his freedom when he accepted the cause in the name of which he carries out his acts of oppression. When a man submits to political idealism of the kinds that are opposing each other in the world today he becomes the agent of sub-human, demonic powers. That is why, as Gabriel Marcel says in *Men Against Humanity*:

> "Today, the first and perhaps the only duty of the philosopher is to defend man against himself: to defend man against that extraordinary temptation towards inhumanity to which—almost always without being aware of it—so many human beings today have yielded."[4]

It is the duty of the philosopher, the artist and of every individual man to establish within himself that condition of freedom which will enable him to think independently. And the most effective way of doing this is for each man to rediscover God for himself. Otherwise there can be no escape from the tyranny of the "isms", from the state of affairs in which the killer fears the law more than his own conscience, and in which for the majority of men there exists no absolute and imperative code of values or moral principles.

At a time like the present, when tremendous psychological forces are at work reducing men to a common level, religion alone can save the individual human personality from submergence. By this I do not mean that the Church can do it, but rather that a man having a genuine religious attitude to life will be immune to the levelling process. Such an attitude does not involve merely the acceptance of a number of beliefs, but is an active relationship between the human personality and the Divinity. "God can no more do without us than we can do without him"[5] says Eckhart, and it is this sense of a *dynamic* relationship between man and God that is missing from much modern religion. D. H. Lawrence rebelled against the religion of his youth because he felt that it was devoid of spirituality, did not involve any of man's higher faculties. Living in his early years in a Midland mining town, he was in close contact with the stagnant, unimaginative bourgeois mentality which he came to hate so in his later life. This word "bourgeois" has been bandied about vituperatively for some decades now, but it remains a fact that there has developed since the Industrial Revolution a distinct type of mentality, particularly, but by no means exclusively, among the so-called "middle classes". No doubt it existed before, but during the last two centuries it has spread with unprecedented rapidity. It is this mentality that has reduced religion to church attendance and hymn-singing, and against it every true religious man has revolted. Its development was the cause of the artist's alienation from his fellow-men. Subjective religion is the only antidote for this insidious force, the only thing that can attack it at its roots in the human psyche. Contrary to the belief of many people, it is the religious attitude that makes possible the development of the individual personality. By living a rich and intense intellectual and imaginative life, man maintains and develops his personality and keeps open within himself the way to the Absolute.

In the nineteenth century the artist took a healthy pleasure in fighting against the bourgeois, but as the century progressed the struggle became more and more vain. The *fin de siècle* poets in France, who are now usually grouped together under the name of "the Symbolists", were the first group to choose deliberately to detach themselves from the life of their time. The increasing materialism of the world around them severed these artists from society and drove them to believe it their duty to maintain *within themselves* a right standard of values. Thus emerged the great individualist visionaries, Rimbaud, Proust, Joyce, Rilke and Yeats, all of them proudly religious artists and all of them unable to find in Christianity a symbolism adequate for what they had to say. Each had to develop in his own work a private symbolism, and this added to the obscurity of his work and further limited its appeal. The incompatibility which the artist felt between his ideals and the ideals of society had forced him into the position of an "outsider". If he was at all concerned with the salvation of society he could only conceive that salvation to be possible by the general adoption of his ideals. This, of course, was impossible, and all he ultimately effected was the salvation of himself.

We cannot criticise this literature as mere escapism. If it were nothing more than that these authors would be of no more significance to us today than Swinburne is. They remain significant because their dilemma is one with which each individual artist is still faced today. Their example teaches us the advantages and disadvantages of the two alternative ways : to be detached and thus enable the unfettered spirit to express itself freely ; or to involve oneself in the fate of the world, do what one can to save it, though at the expense of admitting impure elements into one's work and not realising to the full one's potentialities as an artist. Joyce, Rilke and the rest did the world the invaluable service of keeping alive the religious standard of values. It was their integrity and absolute dedication to their art that enabled them to do this. But, on the other hand, Thomas Mann has reminded us that "In our time the destiny of man presents its meaning in political terms".[6] Is it any longer possible for the artist to keep clear of political issues? And if he gets involved in them how is he to avoid the mistakes of the poets of the 'thirties, who, for all their sincerity, are so palpably smaller men than the great visionary individualists? There is a third course open to him, namely the return to Orthodoxy. This would give him the advantage of an absolute and incorruptible set of values, but the Church is alienated from the majority of the human community, and such an action would not provide an answer to the fundamental question of our time, which is : how is the conscientious individual who holds a religious set of values to be right, to relate himself harmoniously to a world whose values are almost entirely materialistic?

Such is the confused world into which the modern artist

c

is born. Each of his alternatives demands of him either a compromise or a sacrifice, so that it seems that while he is destined to pick his way among problems no artist can put on the cloak of greatness which has been handed down the ages since Homer's day. He is not free enough. The greatest beauty of character we can find among modern men is the pride and singleness of purpose, the heroic defiance, of a Joyce or a Yeats.

But amid all the confusion of the last four decades it is possible to pick out a train of development leading, perhaps, out of the maze. This train is an attitude, shared, I think, by a growing number of thinking people. The present book is intended to be, in one of its aspects, a history of this development.

I speak, of course, of the authentic religious attitude outlined in the last chapter. But it is not my personal caprice or my desire to inculcate an attitude to life which I believe to be right and fruitful, that brings me back to this point, so much as the weight of the actual evidence. Before the First World War T. E. Hulme's studies of modern art led him to ask: "May not the change of sensibility, in a region like aesthetics, a by-path in which we are, as it were, off our guard, be some indication that the *humanist tradition is breaking up*—for individuals here and there, at any rate?"[7] And after the war, though Hulme did not live to see it, there appeared further evidence of the break-up of Humanism. The chaos of the 'twenties was largely due to the growing feeling that the old ways of thought were no longer adequate, and also to the fact that the springs of spiritual force, so long inactive, were beginning to bubble up again. *The Waste Land* ends with a religious solution to the modern problem. And it is not only Mr. Eliot's personal solution, but one that he picked, as it were, out of the air of his time. The vision of ugliness, the despair, the ennui in his early poetry, had already stamped Mr. Eliot as potentially a religious man, but it was not until 1922 that he was able to cap his negative vision with a note of affirmation. The question of the lady in the first part of the *Game of Chess* section, "What shall we do tomorrow? What shall we ever do?" echoes the question in Baudelaire's journal: "What, under Heaven, has this world henceforth to do?"[8] There may be many answers to the question, but that of the religious man, the yea-sayer who is not blind to any of the facts, is most likely to penetrate to the root of the matter.

What the world has yet to do has become increasingly obvious to people since the end of the Second World War. Man has to prove himself big enough not to be submerged beneath the deluge released by his own ingenuity. He has liberated tremendous natural forces, now he has to learn to control them. As Jung has remarked, "man is exposed today to the elemental forces of his own psyche".[9] These too, the forces that urge him against his will and against his conscience to war and destruction, he must control. H. G. Wells wrote the following words in *The Open Conspiracy* in the early 1930s, and he was only one of the numerous people who were and are acutely aware of their truth:

"Unprecedented possibilities, mighty problems, we realise, confront mankind today. They frame our existences. The practical aspect, the material form, the embodiment of the modernized religious impulse is the direction of the whole life to the solution of these problems and the realization of their possibilities. The alternative before man now is either magnificence of spirit and magnificence of achievement, or disaster."[10]

In 1956 it is still not clear whether man is going to prove himself equal to the challenge with which the modern world confronts him. Is he big enough? The question remains unanswered. It is no exaggeration to say that the present is a testing-time, a period in which all that man is, all that he has achieved, wrested from nature, is thrown in the balance against "the elemental forces of his own psyche". "Civilisations rise and fall," says the sceptic, but the religious man cannot subscribe to such a mechanical view of history. Civilisations, as Professor Arnold Toynbee has pointed out, have been rising and falling for only the minutest fraction of historical time, and the fact that twenty or so of them have risen and declined according to a roughly similar pattern, does not mean the millions that may yet be to come must inevitably follow an identical pattern. Human life is meaningful only if we can conceive the possibility of man some day reaching the edge of the abyss and then turning back, confounding the forces that would urge him to cast himself into its depths, and entering on a new and higher-level existence. And if that is possible some day, why not today? The challenge of destiny is always a challenge to man's spiritual faculties, though it presents itself in political and economic terms. In our time the crucial challenge is that expressed by the hackneyed phrase "peaceful co-existence". Can man control or harmlessly canalise his instinct for destruction, which, as the psychologists have shown, is deeply bedded in his unconscious? Can he break down the barriers of narrow nationalism and emerge—as he must if he is to survive under prevailing economic conditions—into the brighter day of world unity? In its essential form the question is: will man suffer the complete atrophy of his spiritual faculties, or will he, by exercising them vigorously, bring about the millennium?

The change in sensibility which Hulme observed in art has been paralleled in science and philosophy. The turn of the century brought the first of the many discoveries and theories that were destined to overthrow completely the mechanical view of man and the world which evolutionism and the sciences of the nineteenth century had fostered. In 1900 Max Planck published his Quantum Theory which, in the words of Sir James Jeans, "dismissed continuity from nature, and introduced a discontinuity for which there was so far no evidence".[11]* And after Einstein's Principle of Relativity was published in 1905 "it became clear that the

* "One of the main achievements of the nineteenth century was the elaboration and universal application of the principle of *continuity*. The destruction of this conception is, on the contrary, an urgent necessity of the present."—T. E. Hulme, *Speculations*, p. 3.

phenomena of nature were determined by us and our experiences rather than by a mechanical universe outside us and independent of us."[12] The rationalism of the eighteenth century and the materialism of the nineteenth tottered beneath the pressure of scientific progress in the first decade of the present century. Albert Einstein, who was surely one of the greatest intellects of our time, frequently used the word "God" in his writings. "God is sophisticated," he said, "but he is not malicious."[13] Sophisticated may seem a strange adjective to use in reference to the Deity, but what Einstein meant by the phrase is that the natural world seems to be organized according to the laws of mathematics ; that the Creator, in fact, seems to be a pure mathematician. The difference between the elements is simply a difference in the number of electrons in a single atom, and it is possible to fulfil the dreams of the mediaeval alchemist and change base metal into gold simply by altering its atomic structure. For centuries the atom had been pictured as a minute but solid piece of matter, but when Rutherford devised a means of exploring its interior he made the surprising discovery that it consisted mainly of empty space. If all the solid matter in the human body was compressed together, Sir Arthur Eddington tells us, it would make up a particle of so minute a size that it would only be observable through a microscope. The scientist has certainly taken some of the wind out of man's sails by so diminishing his stature. Today man is no longer the Lord of Creation ; for all we know he may be just an accident of nature, destined to strut around on a speck of dust for a mere few million years and then fade out of existence, while the galaxies, indifferent to his coming and his going, continue their eternal perambulation of space. The discoveries of twentieth-century physical science, though they have vastly increased man's knowledge, have also lessened him in his own eyes ; and they have thus made possible again the religious ideas which the mechanical views of the nineteenth century denied.

For readers who are allergic to metaphysics, even when it is rooted in the solid earth of physical science, there is another modern science which brings us back to a similar position, namely, psychology. Nineteenth century psychologists worked close alongside the anthropologists and were interested in man as a type. In other words their studies were confined to the normal man. Freud and Jung, again in the first decade of this century, became interested in the psychology of the abnormal and made the great discovery that man has an unconscious as well as a conscious mind. Their explorations of this unconscious mind served only to reveal to them its yet unfathomable depths. So psychology, like every other science, brought man face to face with the great unknown, the giant question-mark. The limits of knowledge and speculation have, during the last fifty years, receded rapidly beyond the range of our vision and today the imaginative man is faced with *a void*. If all things are relative all things are equally valueless, and man can only give meaning to his existence by committing himself to an absolute standard of values, however irrational that may be. If a man living in the mid-twentieth century refuses to believe in God because such belief is irrational he shows that his mind is still running in the grooves of the nineteenth-century categories of thought. Science has explored and observed the phenomena of the natural world, but it is powerless to explain *why* things are as they are. Long ago it discovered that reason, in the purely human sense, is not the ruling principle in the universe. But when the scientist rests for a moment from his task of observing and exploring and attempts to comment on the results of his researches, the most he can do is to admit, humbly and reverently, that "God is sophisticated".

One of the most important and most misunderstood movements in thought in our time is the one generally known as "existentialism". In the popular mind the term is too closely associated with the name of Jean-Paul Sartre. Sartre, by reason of his talents as a dramatist and novelist has tended in recent years to command more attention than the other existentialist philosophers. But existentialism had its origin in the Christian thought of Kierkegaard and since his day it has been its purpose *to keep open the way to the Absolute in the face of the materialism of the modern world*. Of these philosophers Mr. F. H. Heinemann says: "Their point of departure is the fact and problem of alienation, their aim the liberation from estrangement."[14]

Existentialism is a movement of religious thought and that is why it has not produced, and cannot produce, a philosophical system. It is not concerned with systems, but with the problems of human existence. In different ages philosophy serves different functions, and in our time it cannot keep clear of the problems of living. Many of the philosophers of the past excluded personal factors from their work, but for the existentialists personal factors are all-important. "Truth is subjectivity" declared Kierkegaard, and the statement is a curious anticipation of the Relativity theory, which, as Sir James Jeans says, took the emphasis off the objective world outside us "and retransferred it to us and our subjective measurements".[15]

Heidegger is the supreme example of the existentialist in rebellion against the philosophy of the past. He rejects logic as the necessary basis of philosophy and overturns the whole applecart of traditional philosophy from Aristotle to Descartes. He and the other existentialist thinkers reject most of the problems of the traditional school as pseudo-problems, and declare that the only real problems are those which are intimately connected with human existence. Existence cannot be systematised, it is a living, changing thing, and once you begin analysing it or talking about it in a detached, theoretical manner, you falsify it. As T. E. Hulme writes: "Philosophical syntheses and ethical systems are only possible in armchair moments. They are seen to be meaningless as soon as we get into a bus with a dirty baby and a crowd".[16] Karl Jaspers is perhaps the most detached of the existentialist philosophers, but even he confesses, "I must die, I must suffer, I must struggle, I involve myself inexorably in guilt".[17]

It will be clear, I hope, that existentialism is not one of those eccentric fashions that come and go in the intellectual world, but represents a heroic effort of the human mind, in the full possession of its highest faculties, to confront the problems of existence in the modern world. These problems are seen in different terms by each of the thinkers to whom the word "existentialist" has been applied, but fundamentally they are the same. They are the problems of a religiously-inclined individual trying to live fully and meaningfully under the social and intellectual conditions which prevail today. What unites the existentialist thinkers is a certain condition of mind, an attitude to modern circumstances and problems. Christian or atheist, they are all committed to the same task : to defend the rights of the individual against all "isms", all collective movements, particularly Communism and Fascism. They hold the individual human personality to be paramount, and resist all tendencies that might lead to a depersonalisation and despiritualisation of man. It is their object to free man from the dominion of powers which prevent him from realising the fullness of his personality, to make it possible for him to live an authentic existence.

I said above that the problems of existentialism are those of the religiously-inclined individual. Now it is quite obvious in what sense the Christian existentialists, Kierkegaard, Berdyaev, Marcel, even Jaspers, may be called religious, but what is not so obvious is how the term could be applied to Sartre, Husserl and Heidegger. Nevertheless, I wish to maintain that all existentialist thought is religious. It is so because it springs from a distinctly religious attitude to life. Husserl's "One becomes a philosopher through loneliness"[18] is the *cri de cœur* of a man of the Pascalian stamp. The sentence could be used as the epigraph to the work of any of the existentialists, for they are all "outsiders", solitary men who have beheld the unstable foundations of human life, the chaos beneath the apparently ordered surface. Heidegger describes the human situation as "being exposed to nothingness",[19] and in both his and Sartre's work the reality of ultimate nothingness is profoundly realised and courageously faced. Sartre makes no attempt to divert his attention from the absurdity of human existence, and because of this he has obtained for himself a reputation as a philosopher of negativity. Such he is, but there are in his writings definite moral implications. Like Rilke he seeks to affirm not-being, to make it contiguous with being, to contain it within the realm of being. In *The Republic of Silence* he tells how during the German occupation, when they were faced at every moment and on all sides with the possibility of not-being, he and his colleagues in the resistance movement realised as never before their *freedom*. When he defines freedom as "total responsibility in total solitude"[20] we realised that he is not referring to external freedom, but to the freedom of the spirit. In fact he is saying exactly the same thing as I expressed earlier in this chapter in the words: "Man achieves his highest possible degree of freedom when he stands personally responsible for his actions before God". Sartre may be an atheist, but his vision of the ultimate reality behind the appearances of life, his courage in the face of not-being, his reiterated injunction that man must "commit himself", all mark him as a profoundly religious man.

Implicit in existentialism is a philosophy of redemption. Behind the work of all these thinkers there is a desire to restore to man the *breadth of existence* which he has unsuspectingly lost in the conditions of modern life. The unauthentic existence of many individuals living in a machine-age, and themselves becoming mechanical in their thinking and their way of responding to situations, must be replaced by the meaningful, authentic existence of the spiritual life. First in Germany, then in France and Italy, existentialism arose in the wake of national disasters; it was the last outpost of the spirit, which, in the face of the degeneration of all values, issued its warning and its message of hope to those who had ears to hear.

In the situation of the existentialist thinkers is mirrored the fundamental paradox of human existence in our time. They wish to keep intact the authenticity of their own existence and at the same time have a deep need to communicate with others, to relate themselves to the world. Once already in this chapter I have asked how this can be done, but no

simple answer is forthcoming. The problem of man's alienation from himself, from his fellow-men and from God can
only be solved by each individual in his solitude. So now is
the time for us to turn to a consideration of individual poets.
This first part of the book has, I hope, provided a psychological and historical background which will enable the
reader to regard these poets not as isolated individual artists,
but as men of different psychological constitution susceptible
in various degrees to the forces and problems which frame
the life of modern man.

PART TWO

PART TWO

CHAPTER ONE

DYLAN THOMAS AND THE RELIGION OF THE INSTINCTIVE LIFE

"Man's world is no more nature. It is hell
Made by Man-self of which Man must grow well."[1]

STEPHEN SPENDER

I

THE RELIGIOUS LIFE, as we have seen, consists in a quest for unity, for a release from the limits of selfhood and a participation in some larger life which invests the particular individual life with meaning. This unity can be realised on a number of different levels. Many men find it by pursuing the life of instinct. Behind what D. H. Lawrence called the "cerebral consciousness" of modern man, deep down in his unconscious mind, lies the matrix of life itself, a condition of being whereon all things share a mystical common identity. Lawrence believed that if a man could draw the sap of his daily existence from these roots, if, in other words, he could direct his life uninhibitedly according to the dictates of instinct, he would break through all the pettiness and superficiality which has accumulated like a crust on the life of modern man. Thereby he would realise an authentic existence.

Lawrence was a dialectician and what he preached was the practice of the poet Dylan Thomas. When he was not catching queer fish in the stream of the unconscious, Thomas was singing the praises of the instinctive life. His finest poems are those in which he conveys a feeling of man's co-existence with nature. His radio play *Under Milk Wood* describes the life of a Welch fishing village from sunrise to nightfall, and his characters, brilliant and authentic though they are, never come out of the dream state of unconscious existence. Life proceeds guided by the rhythm of the rising and setting of the sun, and not one of the inhabitants of the village is able, by an act of will, to assert man's autonomous existence, his independence of nature. Nature, the mother of all, broods over all the poems Thomas wrote, and shelters man with her dark wing. In a note to his *Collected Poems* Thomas said that they were written "for the love of Man". No doubt they were, but Man is as variously interpreted a word as God. Man, in fact, is not present in Dylan Thomas's poetry. The lusting blood, the dreaming unconscious mind are present; but man the creator, the being fully conscious of his high destiny, is an alien figure.

D. H. Lawrence always stood apart from the literary movements of his day. He regarded such poets as Rilke and Eliot as too intellectual, over-cultivated to the point of ignoring the primal elements in the constitution of the human animal. We shall have to consider this criticism in the chapters devoted to these poets, but here we might justifiably ask whether Lawrence's emphasis on the physical fact did not result in his committing the fault for which he criticised others, the fault of presenting only one aspect of human life to the exclusion of other equally important aspects. The same question could be asked about Dylan Thomas. Thomas never expressed in print his attitude towards his contemporaries. He was content to be a poet in his own way and to allow others the same liberty. And his way was different from the prevailing fashions of the time. He was never an intellectual poet. His glorification of the instinctive life came from within him; given his psychological constitution it was inevitable. It was not, as with Lawrence, conceived as a panacea for the present ills of society. In fact Thomas was as little concerned with society as he was with the poets who were his contemporaries. But although in his lifetime he stood apart from his contemporaries, in the eyes of posterity he will stand alongside them, for he lived in the same world, was influenced by the same conditions and experienced the same problems. In his poetry there is implied a distinct attitude towards these problems, and to life generally, which criticism will abstract from its literary context and compare with the attitudes of Rilke, Eliot and other poets who were so different from him.

Dylan Thomas has come nearer than anyone else in recent years to being a popular poet. We cannot ignore this fact; it compels us to ask whether his attitude is not more valid for modern man than that of the more intellectual poets. But first we must decide whether that attitude represents a confrontation of or an escape from the problems of existence. The phrase "the problems of existence" is to be taken in a dual sense throughout this book. It refers both to the particular problems of the individual living in the modern world and the eternal problems encountered by man when, face to face with destiny, he poses the metaphysical questions of his own and God's nature and the purpose of life. Putting aside literary standards of judgment for a time, we shall take Dylan Thomas as an example of the psychological type whose religion is that of the instinctive life. We will then try to discover to what extent this attitude fulfils the functions of a religion, which are to give to man a sense of meaningful existence, of unity with a higher, divine principle, and, above all, a vision of the ultimate truth and reality which lies behind appearances.

II

One of the truest things ever said about Dylan Thomas was said by himself when he began one of his early poems with the line

"I, in my intricate image, stride on two levels."

The one level, he said, was that of the "brassy orator", and the other that of "my half ghost in armour"—an image which may be translated prosaically as "my spirit imprisoned in flesh." Of course we all move, not only on two, but on several levels of existence, but with most of us the contrast is not so great as it was in Dylan Thomas between the wild, loud-mouthed, drunken Celt and the painstaking poetic craftsman. Thomas, the libertine, made excellent copy for the journalists and made quite a reputation for that other man, Thomas the poet. When he died, the Thomas legend, which had been growing slowly during the last years of his life, chanced to capture the public imagination and he was elevated to the position of Popular Poet No. 1.

The legend of "fierce, fine and foolish Thomas, poet, roisterer and lover of mankind," as one popular journalist described him, is a falsification of the facts for it ignores an important aspect of the man's character—his weakness. The Celt often hides his true self beneath a mantle of his own fashioning, and very often his brilliance, boastfulness, wildness and bravado conceal an inability to deal with life and to shape his own destiny. Dylan Thomas's finest poems are a triumph over his native weakness of character. He himself has told how he had to labour over them to give them such permanence as they may possess. In such a way he created some half-dozen perfect and immortal poems—an achievement sufficient to absolve any man.

I do not mention the poet's weakness in order to slight his character. It is a psychological fact, and as such not open to criticism. I mention it here because in his use of language there is a certain imaginative vigour, and in his attitude to death a simple courage, which gives the impression of his being a man of strong character. What strength he had resulted from the simplicity of his vision. He was a poet of faith, and it is in those simple but subtly-wrought poems in which he affirms his faith that he is at his best. Faith came easily to him, but it did not come often ; at least the passionate faith that gave birth to *Poem in October*, *A Winter's Tale*, *Fern Hill*, and *A Refusal to Mourn the Death, by Fire, of a Child in London*, was the exception rather than the rule with him. It was a transfigured Dylan Thomas who wrote these poems, quite a different man from the legendary figure, who, though he would not be dictated to by men or the institutions of men, was nevertheless a slave to his instincts and suffered from that indetermination which is characteristic of his brilliant race.

Yet in a way the two beings who inhabited the body beneath Dylan Thomas's grubby fisherman's jersey were not so contradictory. The one lived, the other celebrated, the instinctive life. I have already stated that he was a poet of faith, and he himself said that his poems were written "in praise of God", but now we must examine these statements a little more carefully. What were the attributes of the God whom Thomas celebrated in his poems? Certainly he was not a stickler for morality. Indeed, Thomas's religious attitude may be compared with that of primitive man in the ages before moral concepts became associated with religion. Nor was he an ideal, if we are to understand by that word a Being, conceived as perfect, towards whom human effort is orientated. Dylan Thomas's god had little in common with the God of the Christians. He demanded no sacrifice of man. No particular effort of will was required in order to attain to the condition of unity with him. Only a complete absorption in the life of the senses :

"And taken by light in her arms at long and dear last
        I may with fail
    Suffer the first vision that set fire to the stars"

says the poet at the end of *Love in the Asylum*. Here is a doctrine which directly contradicts the tested truth of all the great religions, that man can only attain to union with God by the complete submission of his own will and the purification of the soul which follows the suppression of the sensual appetites. The contradiction disappears when we realise the two quite different gods are involved. The great gods of the world are transcendent as well as immanent, and they are apprehended by man's conscious mind. The god of Dylan Thomas is wholly immanent, felt along the bloodstream or in the sexual organs, buried in the unconscious. He possesses no attributes, is capable neither of love nor anger, but is conceived rather as a vague Force or Power which is responsible for the harmony of the world and is most clearly discernible in that harmony.

Pantheism has its place in all religions, but it does not constitute a religion in itself because it gives man nothing to live by. It provides neither a code of conduct nor a solution to the question of the goal of life. Nevertheless, people who are not given to metaphysical questioning find it sufficient for their needs, and indeed more congenial than the genuine religions which demand sacrifices of them. However, pantheism is not a word which covers one easily definable attitude to life. Generally speaking, it represents the belief or feeling that all creation has a common identity because all things are manifestations of God. But men may arrive at such a belief in various ways and act upon it differently. Most pantheists are content to exult in the feeling of a mystical and harmonious relationship existing between themselves and the natural world. A few, not content to be identified with the part, seek the whole, and try to be at one with God, the fountain-head of all. Such was the endeavour of the mystic Jacob Boehme, who made a penetrating observation, though one with which most pantheists would disagree, when he wrote: "If thou wilt be like all things, thou must forsake all things ; thou must turn thy desire away from them all."[2]

Dylan Thomas's pantheism directly contradicted this statement of Boehme's. Far from forsaking all things, Thomas found that the complete absorption in the particular which attends sexual union was for him the gateway to the unitive life. It led him into the depth of the unconscious, a sticky world where blindly the life force pursued its task of genesis. Genesis was the predominant theme in his first published volume, *Eighteen Poems*. That is partly the reason why much of his early work is obscure : in attempting to probe into the mystery of life, to apprehend biological life at the moment of its first stirring, he had recourse to almost impenetrable imagery. He viewed not only man, but the whole of the natural world, in sexual terms. A process analogous to the human sexual relationship was responsible for the harmony in nature, and indeed in the cosmos. *In the beginning* is a poem in which he gives a symbolically sexual

account of the creation of the universe. Though in his later
work he developed a wider range of subject matter, the
habit of describing things in sexual terms never left him,
and in one of his very last poems we find the lines :

> "At last the soul from its foul mousehole
> Slunk pouting out when the limp time came ;
> And I gave my soul a blind, slashed eye,
> Gristle and rind, and a roarers' life,
> And I shoved it into the coal black sky
> To find a woman's soul for a wife."

If we say that Dylan Thomas was wholly preoccupied
with sex we are in danger of giving the wrong impression
that he was an erotic poet. He was in fact far less erotic than
D. H. Lawrence. His attitude to sex, in his poetry at any
rate, was almost clinical. Sex was for him the overwhelming
mystery. Without it no living thing could overcome its
separateness ; by it all things were made as one. Whereas
the pantheist normally sees God in all things, Thomas saw
sex in all things. In fact sex, together with the processes
analogous to it in the natural world, was Dylan Thomas's
god. The sexual act between man and woman was therefore
invested with a grave significance. The act that created life
was symbolical of the moment of death ; for death was the
entry into the womb of the universe, and as man and woman
surrender their separate identities at the moment of union,
so does man give up his identity when submerged by death.

Dylan Thomas's attitude to death was similar to that of
Shelley when he wrote on the death of Keats in *Adonais* that
"He is made one with nature." One of Thomas's finest
poems celebrates this fact :

> "And death shall have no dominion.
> Dead men naked they shall be one
> With the man in the wind and the west moon ;
> When their bones are picked clean and the clean bones
>   gone,
> They shall have stars at elbow and foot ;

Though they go mad they shall be sane,
Though they sink through the sea they shall rise again ;
Though lovers be lost love shall not ;
And death shall have no dominion."

Death was a return to the matrix of life, to the

> "mankind making
> Bird beast and flower
> Fathering and all humbling darkness."

The darkness of which Thomas speaks is different from that
meant by T. S. Eliot in the two lines from *East Coker* : "I
said to my soul, be still, and let the dark come upon you/
Which shall be the darkness of God". Thomas's darkness is
not the darkness of God, but rather that of the unconscious
mind. Out of that darkness man emerges into consciousness,
and when the brief span of his life is completed he returns
to it. For what purpose he emerges and what he accomplishes
during the period of consciousness, are questions the poet
never asked. The implication in his poetry seems to be that
man fulfils his function in this life at those moments when
he absorbs himself in nature and thus returns to the state of
pristine unconsciousness.

Death is one of the major themes in Dylan Thomas's
poetry. The first impression we get from reading his more
popular and easily understandable works is that he is a perfectly healthy-minded writer. But on reading him with more
attention we are forced to reconsider our first impression
when we come across lines like :

> "I sit and watch the worm beneath my nail
> Wearing the quick away."

or

> "I smell the maggot in my stool."

or

"When, like a running grave, time tracks you down".

It is notable that all these lines appear in his first volume of
poems. In 25 Poems he wrote Death shall have no dominion,
and in Deaths and Entrances, his third and last volume, a
serene and reconciled Poem on his Birthday. It is as though
in his second book he became more confirmed in his
pantheistic faith. His poetic starting-point was an attempt
to get to "the sensual root and sap" of life. He discovered
that it was a force of dynamic attraction operative in
the human animal in the form of the sexual instinct.
This force manifested itself in all living things. When he
wrote :

"The force that through the green fuse drives the flower
  Drives my green age ; that blasts the roots of trees
  Is my destroyer."

he had already taken the easy and natural step from his
original position to that of the pantheist. But, as the
second part of the quoted lines shows, he was not yet
reconciled to the fact of mutability and death. Perhaps
the impact of the war brought from him the affirmation
that "Death shall have no dominion," a statement which
he confirmed with the sonorous last line of the magnificent Refusal to Mourn the Death, by Fire, of a Child in
London :

"After the first death, there is no other."

By the time he came to write the poems which were published in Deaths and Entrances the note of morbidity had
quite disappeared from Thomas's poems about death. It
was replaced first by the promethean defiance of Do not go
gentle into that good night, then by the joyful acceptance which
found expression in one of his last poems, namely, Poem on
his birthday :

" . . . the closer I move
To death, one man through his sundered hulks,
    The louder the sun blooms
And the tusked, ramshackling sea exults;
    And every wave of the way
And gale I tackle, the whole world then,
    With more triumphant faith
Than ever was since the world was said,
    Spins its morning of praise,
    I hear the bouncing hills
Grow larked and greener at berry brown
    Fall and the dew larks sing
Taller this thunderclap spring, and how
    More spanned with angels ride
The mansouled fiery islands! Oh,
    Holier than their eyes,
And my shining men no more alone
    As I sail out to die."

Equally important as, and in a way complementary to, the theme of death, there runs through Dylan Thomas's poetry another theme: that of pre-natal life. Coupled with the genesis theme it was predominant in *18 Poems*. It is perhaps expressed most clearly in the poem *Before I knocked and flesh let enter*, where the condition of pre-natal life is described in terms similar to those used when he speaks of life after death.

Dylan Thomas's mind had no metaphysical proclivities, otherwise he would have been obliged to find an answer to the question, Why does man proceed from a state of absorption in nature through earthly life and then back to the same state? Preoccupied as he was with the phenomenon of life, he never had time to ask questions about it. With the problems which we shall see tormenting the minds of other poets dealt with in this book he was blissfully unconcerned. He arrived at the paradise of faith without passing through the hell of despair or the purgatory of doubt. He saw man's situation in the universe in the simplest terms. And his own position too was clear to him : he was here to sing the glory of life. When he was not probing into the unconscious he became what he really was : a bard in the old sense of the word, a descendant of Chaucer or Villon or of his own great mediaeval compatriot Dafydd Ap Gwilyn. His lack of interest in metaphysical issues was responsible at once for his limitations and for his greatness. His simple vision invested his poems with a certain grandeur and enabled him to divine what Hopkins called "the freshness deep down things."

As he grew older Dylan Thomas seemed to recapture the undivided consciousness of the child or the animal. His relationship with nature was one of immediate response. There are no Wordsworthian mystical overtones in his poems. Nature-mysticism is only possible for a civilised mind. It is a means of bridging a gap between man and nature which was non-existent for primitive man. For Thomas, too, such a gap did not exist. On his thirtieth birthday he rose early and went from the town into the country, where he had passed the days of his youth. And there he remembered that :

> "These were the woods the river and sea
> Where a boy
> In the listening
> Summertime of the dead whispered the truth of his joy
> To the trees and the stones and the fish in the tide.
> And the mystery
> Sang alive
> Still in the water and singingbirds."

"The mystery sang alive still" : never throughout his life did Dylan Thomas lose the freshness and immediacy of the child's vision of nature. In most men the sense of wonder is blunted by the passing years and the capacity for delight diminished. Not so with this poet. With Thomas Traherne he could have said :

"I seemed as one brought into the Estate of Innocence. All things were spotless and pure and glorious : yea, and infinitely mine, and joyful and precious. I knew not that there were any sins, or complaints or laws. . . . I was entertained like an Angel with the works of God in their splendour and glory, I saw in all the peace of Eden ; Heaven and Earth did sing my Creator's praises, and could not make more melody to Adam, than to me."[3]

For Thomas everything in the natural world was infinitely his, for, living on the level of the instinctive life, he felt no barrier between himself and that life in its other manifestations.

Thomas, like D. H. Lawrence, was surrounded in his youth by a debased form of Protestant Christianity, and, also like Lawrence, he rebelled against it. Christian teaching was for him a "spent lie" from which he wished to dissociate himself. Yet he was by nature a man of faith and for that reason he was far less capable than Lawrence of completely rejecting Christianity. He wrote :

"I have longed to move away but am afraid ;
    Some life, yet unspent, might explode
    Out of the old lie burning on the ground,
    And, crackling into the air, leave me half-blind."

So his religion became a personal one, a blending of his indigenous paganism and those aspects of Christianity which he found acceptable. In the poem *Find meat on bones*, which appeared in his second volume, he declares with typical pagan pride and high spirits

"War on the destiny of man !
    Doom on the sun !"

but in the very next line, the last one of the poem, there is a sudden reversal of thought, and, either frightened by the

vehemence of his cursing or suddenly becoming aware of
his own insignificance, he says to himself :

"Before death takes you, O take back this."

Such poems are rare in Dylan Thomas's work. As a rule his
poems have neither development nor conclusion, but consist
of a series of images grouped around a central mood or
feeling.

It was while writing his second volume, *25 Poems*, that
Thomas finally determined his attitude towards Christianity
and moved towards that assured personal faith which was to
stamp some of the poems in *Deaths and Entrances* with the
seal of immortality. Throughout his first two books of
poems the themes of time's irrevocable passage and death's
inexorable approach constantly recur. It was this fear of
death which kept him bound to Christianity, even though
he longed to move away from it. He admits the fact in the
first line of one of his more obscure poems :

"It is the sinners' dust-tongued bell claps me to churches."

We have seen how his attitude to death gradually changed,
and as it did so he moved further away from the Christian
attitude to life, which he could never find congenial, and
became more confirmed in his pantheism.

Unconcerned as he was with religion in the moral sense,
Dylan Thomas was unable to appreciate the full significance
of the dogma of original sin. Occasionally he alluded to it,
but if we examine the poems in which he does so we find
that his interpretation of the dogma is unorthodox. It is,
however, quite consistent with his character. It is just what
we might expect from a person whose religion is that of
instinctive life. Of course, he appreciates that there existed
before the Fall a state of innocence in which man lived
unconsciously in harmony with nature. In just such a state
he lived himself, and he is eloquent in speaking of it as :

the morning
Of man when
The land
And
The
Born sea
Praised the sun
The finding one
And upright Adam
Sang u p o n origin!

But when he attempted to describe the cause of the Fall, as
he does in the poem *Incarnate Devil* in *25 Poems*, he signi-
ficantly changes the Christian account of it. According to
Thomas there was no original sin, no momentous human
action which transgressed for the first time the laws of
nature. The change came about without human agency
when

the garden gods
Twined good and evil on an eastern tree."

The knowledge of the distinction between good and evil was
indeed a consequence of the Fall, but its cause was not an
accident as Thomas seems to suggest, but a deliberate
human *action*. Man chose to emerge from the state of unconscious goodness that he might himself be like a god, and,
blessed and cursed with consciousness, might lord it over
the other living creatures and over the material world. By
denying that it was an action on man's part that effected
the change, Thomas missed the whole point. It is because
he deliberately chose to taste of the forbidden fruit of the
tree of knowledge that man is responsible for all the sins of
the world and is burdened with the task of atoning for those
sins and of winning through to that higher state of consciousness which is a second "Estate of Innocence". Dylan
Thomas did not believe in any such higher state of consciousness; for him the greatest imaginable felicity lay in never

emerging from the pristine state of unconscious and instinctive participation in the life of nature. He said so much in one of his last poems, *In Country Sleep*, where the phrase "country sleep" represents the condition of man before the dawn of consciousness :

"The country is holy : O bide in that country kind,
                 Know the green good,
 Under the prayer wheeling moon in the rosy wood
 Be shielded by chant and flower and gay may you
 Lie in grace."

Tracing the course of Dylan Thomas's poetic development, we detect an increasing tendency towards objectivity. The probing into the unconscious of *18 Poems* and the self-questioning of *25 Poems* were succeeded by the radiant outward vision of the best poems in *Deaths and Entrances*. When he died he was beginning to turn his attention to dramatic writing, a field in which his exuberant spirit, his feeling for life and his lively sense of humour served him well. He was a humanist with an eye quick to perceive and to note those superficial idiosyncrasies of human character which are the stuff of popular drama. Mr. Donald Taylor, whose idea it was to write a film scenario about the Burke and Hare murders, states in his Introduction to *The Doctor and the Devils* that he "had been searching for some years to find a story which would pose the question of 'the ends justifying the means.' " It was no less a subject than that which had inspired Dostoevsky's *Crime and Punishment*, but when Dylan Thomas came to write the scenario he neglected this moral issue entirely. The result was a very colourful and entertaining piece of dramatic writing, but far less important a drama than might have been written if the author had concentrated more on the situation of Dr. Rock, who knowingly paid money for murdered corpses in order to advance medical science, than on the two loutish, stupid and uninteresting murderers, Fallon and Broom.

Thomas wrote always out of a sense of delight. Sometimes

it was only delight in the sound of words, as in much of his obscurer poetry where we often feel that he has sacrificed sense to sound; in his best poems it was delight in nature and in his own feeling of identity with it that inspired him; in his dramatic writings it was delight in human character and in his own irrepressible sense of humour. Delight abounds in his writings and humbles the critic who might approach him too academically. His attitude to life and its problems may appear to some of us to be too facile, but we must remember that it developed naturally out of his psychological and physical constitution. And whatever criticism may be levelled against him there will always remain something quite beyond criticism: the perfection of *Fern Hill* and *Poem in October* and the assured mastery of poetic craftsmanship which he revealed in writing *A Winter's Tale* and *In Country Sleep*.

III

What can we say now of general relevance about the type of religious experience which this poet represents? Is the religion of the instinctive life the panacea that Lawrence imagined it to be? Does it satisfy a man's needs on all levels of his being? What effect does it have on his thought and on his capacity for apprehending an ultimate reality? I have already hinted at the answers to some of these questions; it remains for these to be enlarged upon and for the advantages and limitations of the religion of the instinctive life to be comprehensively reviewed.

It is conscious man who has conquered the world of matter and bent it to his purpose, who with the sciences developed by his intellect has explored the microcosm and the macrocosm and released the mighty forces which for so long had lain dormant in nature. If those forces now threaten to overwhelm him he cannot find an escape by attempting to return to his original state of unconscious co-existence with nature. His only hope of salvation lies in his raising himself to a higher state of consciousness, which involves a profounder understanding of himself and of the universe in which he lives. An individual may find his needs best satisfied by the religion of the instinctive life, but he will not find therein any positive solution either to his own or to mankind's problems. He will declare with Thomas that

"What's never known is safest in this life"

and seek to avoid knowledge and thought lest he should burden himself with too heavy a sense of responsibility. In such a condition he will probably live and die happily, but he will not contribute one iota to man's great work of winning from nature, from unconsciousness, a little ground which may henceforth partake of the singular nature of conscious human existence.

Nature is a great balm and comfort to man, and there undoubtedly exists a certain *rapport* between it and important aspects of our own being. Granted that the condition of being alienated from it is bad, but to be wholly immersed in it is equally bad. Man pursues his life, when he lives it fully, on two levels, whereas the life of nature is on one level and is a monotonous affair. The eternal alternation of the seasons and of day and night is quite meaningless unless man is there to give it meaning. It is just those things which distinguish him from other forms of natural life that constitute man's greatness, and that establish a relationship between himself and the God of the higher religions, whom he apprehends not only with his instinctive faculties but with his mind.

The life of instinct obliterates personality. Personality does not consist in superficial peculiarities, but in those triumphs of a man's moral character over his natural self which are the distinctive features of his manhood. When he lives in the security of instinct his latent potentialities are forced into abeyance. He fails to realise himself as a man. He lives without problems and without that tension which urges man to create beyond himself. But the problems remain : the metaphysical problems of human existence and its relationship with time, the universe, and with God, and the practical or political problems of how best to conduct human life on the planet so that it finds conditions conducive to its optimum development. These problems can only be solved by man acquiring a deeper knowledge of himself, which he will do by an effort of consciousness involving the exercise of his higher faculties, and probably aided by the disciplines which have enabled religious men in all lands and ages to free themselves from the tyranny of nature and instinct.

CHAPTER TWO

WALT WHITMAN'S HEALTHY-MINDEDNESS

"Being an individual man is a thing that has been abol-
ished, and every speculative philosopher confuses himself
with humanity at large; whereby he becomes something
infinitely great, and at the same time nothing at all."[1]

KIERKEGAARD

WALT WHITMAN PLACED himself in a position which was
unassailable by criticism. His poems do not purport to be
art, and so the usual criteria of artistic criticism are inapplicable to them. When Henry James reviewed Whitman's
volume of war poems which appeared in 1865 under the
title *Drum-Taps* he wrote that "We find art, measure, grace,
sense sneered at on every page, and nothing positive given
us in their stead. To be positive one must have something
to say; to be positive requires reason, labour, and art; and
art requires, above all things, a suppression of one's self, a
subordination of one's self to an idea. This will never do for
you, whose plan is to adapt the scheme of the Universe to
your own limitations."[2] James speaks truly, and well
expresses the point of view of Whitman's adverse critics,
but his criticism is ineffectual and in a way irrelevant. Like
most Whitman criticism it is the expression of an attitude
to life directly contrary to that of the composer of *Leaves of
Grass*. Whitman, like H. G. Wells, to whom the words
were written, could never have agreed with Henry James
that "it is art that *makes* life, makes interest, makes importance."[3] For him the world was not chaotic, and consequently
the concept of the artist as the man who imposes order upon
chaos, who fashions from the disorderly and meaningless
raw materials of human life something which is perfect,
lasting, and meaningful, was not acceptable to him. The

universe and everything in it, down to the minutest object or living thing, was perfect in Whitman's eyes, he could not wish it different ; and he believed it his glorious task faithfully to mirror that perfection, to make his *Leaves of Grass* a world, a universe, comprehending all, and affirming the goodness of all. That is why he places himself beyond art, regarding himself more as a Prophet in the Hebrew tradition than as an artist in the modern sense. Art is a product of civilization, and Walt Whitman's world is essentially an uncivilized one. "I sound my barbaric yawp over the roofs of the world" he says in *Song of Myself*, fully conscious and indeed proud of the fact that he is not a civilized man. Two contemporaries born so close together could hardly differ more than did Walt Whitman and Henry James. Whitman, believing Western European civilization to be decadent, sought to build up a new civilization in the New World, a Democracy with the ideals of manly love, equality and "Ensemble, Evolution, Freedom". Henry James chose to sink his roots into the European tradition, and while he depicted its decadence he himself remained aloof from it, maintaining his high standards of artistic integrity to the very end. It would be vain to attempt to say which was the greater man, for their paths diverged so widely that there exists between them no common ground for comparison. James, born in New York City, educated in Europe and America, a member of a family in which a dark vision of reality was a common psychological phenomenon,* has

---

* Both his father, Henry James Senior, and his brother William, have recorded accounts of religious experiences which profoundly influenced their lives. In *Society, the Redeemed Form of Man* Henry Senior tells how one day he remained in the room after dinner, gazing into the embers of the fire, "when suddenly—in a lightning flash, as it were, 'fear came upon me, and trembling made all my bones to shake'. To all appearances it was a perfectly insane and abject terror without ostensible cause, and only to be accounted for, to my perplexed imagination, by some damned shape, squatting invisible to me within the precincts of the room, and raying out from his fetid personality influences fatal to life. The thing had not lasted ten seconds before I felt myself a wreck, that is, reduced from a state of firm, vigorous joyful manhood to one of almost helpless infancy." William James's account, disguised

much more in common with the last two poets dealt with in this book than with his compatriot and contemporary Walt Whitman.

Whitman was not by nature inclined towards a dark vision of the world, nor did the circumstances of his life impose one on him. Nineteenth-century America was a virgin land, it did not have behind it irredeemable centuries of bloodshed caused by human power-lust and acquisitiveness. It was a rapidly developing New World, a continent vast and beautiful, lacking a traditional culture but possessing an overpowering sense of its own youthful vigour. It was no place for the fastidious and introspective artist. Its ideals of manhood were those of physical strength and stamina, outspokenness, honesty, cleanness and health. Like most infant communities it had little sympathy with the abnormal, with the man who did not conform to the usual pattern. Its attention was directed outwards, towards material progress and improvement of the conditions of human life. The poetry of Whitman, who became the most representative voice of his epoch, was also an outward-flowing stream. Whitman was not like the artist who works in solitude, and in whom the man who creates, and the man who needs an audience to approve his work, are quite different identities. His poetry needed an audience, the existence of one was a necessary condition of its being

as that of an anonymous "French correspondent" in his *Varieties of Religious Experience*, is strikingly similar to his father's. He tells how on entering a dressing-room one evening, "suddenly there fell upon me without any warning, just as if it came out of the darkness, a horrible fear of my own existence". He too imagined another presence in the room, namely that of an epileptic patient he had seen in an asylum. "There was such a horror of him, such a perception of my own merely momentary discrepancy from him, that it was as if something hitherto solid within my breast gave way entirely, and I became a mass of quivering fear. After this the universe was changed for me altogether. I awoke morning after morning with a horrible dread at the pit of my stomach, and with a sense of the insecurity of life that I never knew before." Such experiences as these are psychological facts. Some people are subject to them, the majority are ignorant of them. Whitman, as always, belonged to the majority, though if he had ever undergone such an experience the whole tone of his writings would have been different.

D

written. The nature of his poetry was to a large extent determined by external circumstances. In time of war he persuaded himself that the one fit theme for the poet was "the theme of war, the fortune of battles, the making of perfect soldiers." When the war was over he declared that it was the function of poetry :

"To exalt the present and the real,
    To teach the average man the glory of his daily walk and
        trade."

In short, Whitman's was propagandist poetry, and he himself admitted this when he wrote in his *Notes on the Meaning and Intention of 'Leaves of Grass'* that : "The whole drift of my books is to form a race of fuller athletic, yet unknown characters, men and women for the United States to come. I do not wish to amuse or furnish so-called poetry, and will surely repel at first those who have been used to sweets and the jingle of rhymes. Then every page of my book emanates Democracy, absolute, unintermitted, without the slightest compromise."

It would be a mistake to leave it at that. Whitman was far more than a propagandist poet. Coming at the time and place that he did he was a very great man, and did much good. On reading him, a man with the most sophisticated sensibilities, though he may wince at his artlessness, cannot fail to find refreshing the great upward surge of natural life which comes from the pages of his book. Truly he said at the beginning of *Song of Myself* : "I permit to speak at every hasard, Nature without check with original energy." This may be opposed to the artistic process of selection and synthesis, but it can produce a kind of literature which transcends art, such as that of the Hebrew Prophets or of Blake in his Prophetic Books. In *Starting from Paumanok* Whitman frankly declared that he wished to inaugurate a religion. He found many followers, and indeed numerous people still respond to that type of natural religion which has been called Whitmanism. His *Leaves of Grass* are therefore not to be judged as poetry, but are to be regarded, more than the work of any other poet represented in this book, purely as the expression of an attitude to life, in fact as religious literature. Such literature, being the expression of psychological states, is not susceptible to criticism, except insofar as one attitude to life can be criticised from the standpoint of another, when both of them are of equal validity.

The aim of Whitman's poetry was to put before his readers a complete world, to give expression to all aspects of life without distinction, to grasp and to express the Whole, without admitting personal preference for any part or personal dislike for any part. Thereby, he hoped to establish contact between the individual who was the reader and the very well-spring of natural life, the source of all energy and goodness. At the end of the second section of *Song of Myself* occur these lines, which may be taken as a statement of the purpose of his poetry :

"You shall no longer take things at second or third hand,
    nor look through the eyes of the dead, nor feed on the
    spectres in books,
You shall not look through my eyes either, nor take things
    from me,
You shall listen to all sides and filter them for yourself."

The presentation of all sides, of life in all its diversity and contradictions, contributes to the work of enlargement which is part of the overall purpose of *Leaves of Grass*. The book has a dual function, of enlargement and union, and the reading of it through imparts a religious experience of a primitive order. Certain poems in the book (*Salut au Monde!* is a typical example), serve the purpose of enlarging the soul of the reader, of taking him out of himself, enabling him to transcend the barriers of space and time, and putting him into relationship with multifarious life. To effect this Whitman adopted the Rabelaisian technique of compiling interminable lists, which sometimes deliberately hold up the

progress of a poem. This process of enlargement is, however, only preparatory to the experience of union, which is
conveyed throughout the book on various levels. Sexual
union is the subject of the poems in the book called *Children
of Adam*, where the poet affirms that "Sex contains all", a
statement with which Dylan Thomas would have agreed.
But sex was not a preoccupation with Whitman, and in his
next book, *Calamus*, he proceeded to advocate the higher
ideal of the union between men on the basis of "manly love".
This type of union is related to the political aspect of his
poetry, for upon this "manly love" would depend the successful functioning of the ideal Democracy that Whitman
envisaged. But Whitman's writings are valuable, not so
much for their political implications, but as a bridge
between the human and the natural worlds, and his most
lasting achievements are those poems in which his nature-
mysticism finds expression, and where the intensity of his
feeling, felicitously captured by his simple and unsophisti-
cated language, conveys to the reader an experience of
union with nature.

Whitman was constantly eulogising the average man,
from whom he differed only by reason of the intensity, and
not the nature, of his feelings. There was nothing extraordinary about his religious experience, it was the common
experience of mankind, only felt more deeply, and consequently occupying a more prominent position in his life,
than is usual with the majority of people. It was the type of
experience I have called psychical, consisting in an apprehension of the essential oneness of the created world and
accompanied by a sense of its ultimate goodness. From this
kind of experience there developed a species of natural
religion, a religion to which the normal, unreflective man,
provided that he does not encounter any great tragedy or
find himself in any extreme situation, might subscribe
throughout the whole of his life. No phrase is more apt
in describing this religious attitude than the one coined
by William James when he spoke of "the religion of
healthy-mindedness". We shall now examine Whitman's

healthy-mindedness under the headings of cosmic consciousness, idea of deity, natural religion, and attitude to
metaphysical issues.

Perhaps Whitman's most typical characteristic is what we
may call his cosmic consciousness. Looking at anything
through Whitman's eyes is like looking through a powerful
magnifying glass ; everything takes on larger proportions by
reason of its participation in the Whole, the cosmos. Everything is endowed with a share in the divine substance, and
therefore there exists a relationship between the soul of man
and all animate and inanimate things. "Having looked at the
objects of the universe," he writes, "I find there is no one
nor any particle of one but has reference to the soul". Whitman had a genius for abstraction, for looking at things in
their general, universal or cosmic aspect. In fact we might
even say that he had no joy in the particular and the concrete except insofar as it opened up for him a beyond of some
sort. That beyond, which was for Whitman the true habitat
of the soul, was the all-enfolding bosom of nature. His attitude to women exemplifies what I mean when I speak of
Whitman's cosmic consciousness. The exuberant sexual
poems in *Children of Adam* give the impression that the
author was a virile man of strong passions. It comes as a
surprise when we read, in the account of him given by his
close friend Peter Doyle to his literary executors, the following words :

> "I never knew a case of Walt's being bothered up by
> a woman. In fact he had nothing special to do with any
> woman except Mrs. O'Connor and Mrs. Burroughs. His
> disposition was different. Woman in that sense never
> came into his head. Walt was too clean, he hated any-
> thing which was not clean. No trace of any kind of
> dissipation in him."

When we think about it, this account is quite consistent with
Whitman's character. Of course he wasn't concerned with
women "in that sense", but only in a general sense. For

him sex was a thing to be celebrated in his poetry first of all because it was natural, and therefore unquestionably good, and secondly because it was a symbol of *merging*, the process which enabled man to participate in the larger life. "A woman waits for me" he announces at the beginning of one of his poems, and before many lines have passed the woman has become "those women that are warm-blooded and sufficient for me". Whitman was constitutionally incapable of keeping himself anchored in the particular. Everything he turned his attention to he regarded in its timeless and universal aspect. Consequently for him the human situation did not appear to be paradoxical or a matter for debate, for he had an unshakable faith that

"All goes onward and outward, nothing collapses,
   And to die is different from what any one supposed, and
      luckier."

In *Song of Myself* Whitman refers to himself as "a kosmos", and says that

"Whoever degrades another degrades me,
   And whatever is done or said returns at last to me."

The desire to contain within himself a whole world, with all its diverse people and places, ideas and occupations, is evident throughout *Leaves of Grass*. "I am integral with you", he says, addressing the sea, and he felt the same about all people he came in contact with: "I do not ask the wounded person how he feels, I myself become the wounded person." Thus his cosmic consciousness was the source and origin of two of his other notable characteristics. Applied to the animal world and the world of inanimate things it produced his nature-mysticism; with regard to the world of man it resulted in an universal sympathy, a belief in the brotherhood of man and the practicability of Democracy.

Cosmic consciousness of the Whitmanic kind is rare in our time. As we noted in the last chapter, modern man's feeling of harmony with nature on one level of his being, namely the unconscious level, is opposed by an awareness of the irreconcilable disparity between the human and natural worlds on another, the intellectual, level. Nevertheless, a kind of cosmic consciousness, a perception that "a vast similitude interlocks all" is a common feature of religious experience, and has, in various ways, affected religious thought. When it is attended by an exalted concept of deity, that is to say a belief in a transcendent God, that God becomes the focal-point for Man's admiration of His works, and, because He is never ultimately knowable, man maintains before Him that humility and selflessness which is an essential precondition to the attainment of truth. When, however, cosmic consciousness exists virtually by itself, when instead of a consciously apprehended God you have a belief in some vague power or influence, man's capacity for praise become diffused throughout the universe, and, in the absence of a defined concept of deity, his faith tends to degenerate into sentimentalism or occultism.

Walt Whitman's idea of deity was neither theistic nor pantheistic, but anthropomorphic. Man was his God. He said so quite straightforwardly in the short poem *Laws for Creations* in *Autumn Rivulets:*

"What do you suppose I would intimate to you in a hundred
        ways, but that man or woman is as good as God?
    And that there is no God any more divine than Yourself?"

His capacity for conveying a sense of the divinity of man is the essence of Whitman's greatness. His poetry imparts to the reader an awareness of the infinite range of potentialities which reside within himself, and stimulates him to surpass himself, morally, artistically, or in whatsoever sphere of activity he is able to do so. The value of such an achievement is not to be underestimated. Man is indeed divine, and awareness of the fact is an incentive to self-transcendence. But his divinity is contained not in his natural self but in his peculiarly human self, that is, in his intellectual activities,

his spiritual apprehensions and his capacity for moral
resolution. Whitman put a rather more mundane interpretation upon the idea of human divinity :

"Divine am I inside and out, and I make holy whatever I
   touch or am touch'd from,
The scent of these arm-pits aroma finer than prayer,
This head more than churches, bibles, and all the creeds."

   For Whitman, God was "the great Camarado". He had
no attributes peculiar to Him as Deity, only those projected
upon Him from the human plane, which were the virtues
the poet most admired in men :

> "Thou, thou, the Ideal man,
>   Fair, able, beautiful, content and loving,
>   Complete in body and dilate in spirit,
>   Be thou my God."

Whitman's God, being completely knowable because completely human, does not provide a point of orientation for
human life or supply an ethic for its conduct. The great gods
of the world are incomprehensible, before them man
becomes aware of his own imperfections and limitations,
which he seeks to transcend by contemplating those Gods.
Faith in the Man-God is only possible for a person who is
blind to man's imperfections, and is untroubled by metaphysical questions. Such a description fits Whitman perfectly. To his mind, concern about the nature of God was a
futile, if not an unhealthy preoccupation :

"And I say unto mankind, Be not curious about God,
   For I who am curious about each am not curious about
      God,
   (No array of terms can say how much I am at peace about
      God and about death.)
   I hear and behold God in every object, yet understand God
      not in the least,
   Nor do I understand who there can be more wonderful
      than myself."

That is plain speaking, it leaves nothing more to be said about Whitman's idea of deity.

All natural religion is healthy-minded. It implies a rejection of the world man has made for himself and an unconditional embracing of the world from which he came, the unconscious world of nature. It has a simple answer to all the problems of existence : follow nature and you cannot go wrong, live in harmony with nature and you will fulfil the purpose of your life, which is, after all, simply to be happy. All of us may at times cry out with Whitman, "give me again O Nature your primal sanities!" But such are moments of weakness, when we neglect our responsibilities to ourselves as human beings, when we succumb to the temptation to find an escape from the demands which implacable Life continually makes upon us. "I see my soul reflected in Nature", says Whitman. So do we all, but what of that other element in the human constitution, the one we have called spirit, where do we see that reflected if not in those things which man accomplishes in despite of nature, whether in the field of art, science, morality or philosophy? It is good to escape from business or politics, from the stupidity and cupidity of men, to the wholesome atmosphere of nature, provided that we remember that nature bears a relationship to but one aspect of ourselves, and that it would be insane to attempt to apply its "primal sanities" to the incommensurable world of human affairs.

In his *Notes on the Meaning and Intention of 'Leaves of Grass'* Whitman wrote : "If the following book does not contain exhaustively within itself, and forever emanate when read, the atmosphere of normal joy and exhilaration which enveloped the making of every part, it will be a failure in the most important respect." To Whitman's mind, which was inclined to over-simplify things, anything abnormal was morbid, whereas the normal was healthy. And for him the norm was the common American Citizen of his day, the labourer, the soldier, or the farmer. In spite of his apparently magnanimous spirit, Whitman's sympathies did not extend far beyond these limits, as his poem in *Drum Taps* addressed

To a Certain Civilian testifies. And if we recall the words of
Peter Doyle we see that Whitman was not as universally
tolerant as he believed himself to be : "Walt was too clean,
he hated anything which was not clean. No trace of any kind
of dissipation in him." To hate anyone or anything for being
what it is is surely quite unwhitmanic. Sooner or later we
must face the fact that Whitman, for all his largeness of
mind, was a puritan. A certain intolerance for dissipation and
weakness is fitting in a religious leader, but only when it is
tempered by an understanding of the psychological cause of
such weakness. To go up to a man who is suffering from the
after-effects of an experience like those recorded by William
or Henry James, and to say to him "Don't be morbid, man,
stand up and take a deep breath of good, clean air," would
be worse than futile. Only the man who has overcome weakness and the tendency to dissipation in himself, who has
seen the darker side of reality, is capable of the sympathetic
understanding which alone justifies intolerance.

The darker side of human experience is quite foreign to
the healthy-minded man. When Whitman says in *Song of
Myself*, "I know the sea of torment, doubt, despair and unbelief" the statement does not ring true. Intellectually he may
have been capable of understanding the torment of doubt,
despair and unbelief, but there is not in his poetry any
evidence that he ever experienced it himself. If he had he
would never have been able to write in the very next section
of that poem the words, "What have I to do with lamentation?" Rilke, with whose nature-mysticism that of Whitman
has certain affinities, admitted that his poetry had its roots
in the dual function of praise and lamentation. For Whitman there was only praise. He was, in his own words, a man
"mad with devouring ecstasy to make joyous hymns for the
whole earth." The absence of the note of lamentation from
his poems, the prevailing optimistic tone of all his writings,
constitute at once his greatness as a singer and his negligible
importance as a thinker.

Healthy-mindedness involves rather more than the belief
that "only health puts you rapport with the universe." When

a man adopts it as a religion demands are made upon it which it is ill-equipped to satisfy. It has to provide a basis for human existence in all its various aspects, to supply a man's intellectual and metaphysical needs as well as his physical ones. It does this in so facile a way that it can only ever attract and hold those whose intellectual and metaphysical needs are very modest. For example, when it is faced with the problem of evil it gets over it simply by denying its reality. "I praise with electric voice," says Whitman, "For I do not see one imperfection in the Universe." Evil, say the healthy-minded, does not exist. What is called evil becomes good when it is regarded in the right way, just as many diseases disappear when you cease to believe in them and practise "faith-healing." The concept of evil is projected upon things by man, and is not inherent in things themselves. The healthy-minded do not go beyond this point to ask, where did man derive his concept of evil from? how did it ever come to exist if not as an explanation of a psychological fact which man observed within himself?

Whitman's attitude to metaphysical issues was one of indifference, bordering sometimes on disdain. "A morning-glory at my window satisfies me more than the metaphysics of books" he says in *Song of Myself*. It is a perfectly consistent healthy-minded attitude. To a man for whom physical life in the world is everything, the preoccupations of the meta-physically-minded seem vain and even morbid. Whitman, delighting greatly in life's journey, never had the inclination to stop and ask where it was leading to. Of course, he saw man as the apex of the created world, but beyond man he saw nothing.

"All forces have been steadily employ'd to complete and
　　delight me,
　Now on this spot I stand with my robust soul."

Where do you go from there? we are inclined to ask. Human life is a constant process of becoming, and a man does not realise himself simply by standing still and admiring his own 'robust soul'.

It would be wrong to say that Whitman was unreflective. The eternal questions did not much concern him, but there were occasions when he doubted, though only momentarily, the reality of things as they appeared. He expresses these doubts in the poem *Of the Terrible Doubt of Appearances* in *Calamus*, but at the end of that poem he reverts to his usual confident self when he is reassured by the physical presence next to him of a friend whom he loves and who holds his hand. For Whitman,

"To be surrounded by beautiful, curious, breathing, laugh-
    ing flesh is enough."

His reflective self was subordinate to his more familiar con-
vivial self and he considered that it was far more healthy and useful to live than to ponder about life. As a poet it was not his business to provide answers to questions, but rather to make people aware of the existence of the questions and stimulate them to ponder them for themselves.

"Let others dispose of questions, I dispose of nothing,
    I arouse unanswerable questions,"

he says in *Myself and Mine*. In this Whitman was wise, for there can be no universal answer to the problems of exist-
ence. The only valid answers are subjective and vary with individuals. Besides, it is not the answers to the problems that matters, so much as the problems themselves. The im-
portant thing is that a man should live in awareness of them, for only then can he live authentically and fully. It is doubtful that Whitman realised this, for he himself did not live in such awareness. It is more likely that his refusal to dispose of questions was simply indicative of a lack of interest in metaphysical issues, attendant upon his preoccupation with life in the physical sense.

Though Whitman's world was the world of man, his under-
standing of the nature of man had serious limitations. First of all he denied man's dual nature, saying "if the body were

not the soul, what is the soul?" It is true that man is an integrated whole, and that if we abstract one of his functions from the rest we are inclined to exaggerate its importance or falsify it in some other way, but it is also true that those who attempt to embrace or conceive man as a whole tend to disregard the paradoxes of his nature, and fail to make the important distinction between his unconscious animal self and his conscious and creative humanity. The developing science of man will eventually prove the idea of duality to be a fiction, but it is a fiction which has afforded man a profounder insight into his own being than the vague belief in himself as an indivisible and wholly good entity.

About the same time as Kierkegaard was issuing his unheeded warnings about "the tyranny of equality", Walt Whitman on the other side of the Atlantic was celebrating in his poems "the divine average". Whitman believed in the equality of men in a sense far wider than the merely political. He was no psychologist, and hardly seems to have understood that men could be constituted differently from himself. He believed that all men had within them the same potentialities and were alike in the manner in which they responded to things. This incapacity for understanding the diversity of human character was one of the most important factors determining the nature of his poetry. It made possible his faith in Democracy, which, as he himself said, emanates from every page of *Leaves of Grass*.

Whitman believed that Democracy was the "purport and aim of all the past." He hoped that it would succeed in

"Scattering for good the cloud that hung so long, that
    weigh'd so long upon the mind of man,
 The doubt and suspicion, dread, of gradual, certain
    decadence of man."

It was a vain hope, for, as time has shown, Democracy in practice has not retarded, but rather accelerated, the decadence of man. Its doctrine of equality and the contributions it has made in other ways to the forwarding of the "levelling process" have tended to take from the individual the consciousness of an elect purpose for himself and to substitute for this a vague ideal of communal purpose. This, I say, is the result, not the intention, of Democracy, a result not very unlike that attained by the practise of the supposedly contrary ideals of Communism.

Given his psychological constitution, it was inevitable that, when he came to turn his attention to political questions, Whitman should discover Democracy. All political systems simplify, and thereby falsify, reality, which is fundamentally anarchic. That is why the genuine religious man keeps clear of them and contents himself with the progress of his own spiritual life and perhaps that of a few chosen disciples. Whitman was simple-minded enough to believe that men were capable of living harmoniously together inspired by some vague ideal of equality and brotherly love. His experiences in the Civil War, when he witnessed many atrocious murders on the field, and many tragic deaths in the hospital, did not shake his faith in the absolute goodness of man. After that war, he believed, men would be transformed, and, inspired by the ideals of Democracy, would live together joyfully and in peace.

"A reborn race appears—a perfect world, all joy !
  Women and men in wisdom innocence and health—all joy !
  Riotous laughing bacchanals fill'd with joy !
  War, sorrow, suffering gone—the rank earth purged—
    nothing but joy left !
  The ocean fill'd with joy—the atmosphere all joy !
  Joy ! joy ! in freedom, worship, love ! joy in the ecstasy of
    life !
  Enough to merely be ! enough to breathe !
  Joy ! joy ! all over joy !"

Subsequent history has made us rather more sceptical about the possibility of peace, and suspicious of the dark forces of man's psyche, so that now Whitman's optimistic lines seem very shallow and unrealistic.

Whitman is of importance to us today in the same way that Nietzsche is. Ironically, he is one of the poets whose influence works against the effects of his own Democratic idealism. Throughout *Leaves of Grass* we continually catch echoes of the Superman theme. For example, in *Song of The Broad-Axe* :

"All waits or goes by default till a strong being appears ;
  A strong being is the proof of the race and of the ability of
    the universe,
  When he or she appears materials are overaw'd,
  The dispute on the soul stops,
  The old customs and phrases are confronted, turn'd back,
    or laid away.
  What is your money-making now? what can it do now?
  What is your respectability now?
  What are your theology, tuition, society, traditions, statute-
    books, now?
  Where are your jibes of being now?
  Where are your cavils about the soul now?"

Those who read Whitman are made aware of their own greatness and nobility as men, and of the existence of a larger life in which they can participate. He made men conscious of themselves, and of the potentialities latent within them, with such lines as :

"The whole theory of the universe is directed unerringly to
  one single individual—namely to You."

The true value of Whitman's poetry resides in the fact that it ennobles and enlarges man in his own eyes ; like Zarathustra's discourses, it impels man to transcend himself. Whitman's prophesies may be proved wrong ; his eclectic religion, requiring of its adherents no act of commitment, may not partake of the features of a genuine and universal religion ; his understanding of human psychology may appear facile, and likewise his denial of the reality of evil ;

the strenuous exclusion from his writings of all the darker aspects of human experience may constitute a falsification of reality : yet, in spite of all these shortcomings, Walt Whitman will surely survive by virtue of his high idealism and his capacity for conveying to men a sense of their own divinity.

CHAPTER THREE

W. B. YEATS: THE DIVIDED MAN

"The significance of man's outlook varies according as he sunders himself into spirit and flesh, into understanding and sensuality, into soul and body, into duty and inclination—also into his being and its phenomenal aspect, into his actions and his thoughts, into what he actually does and what he thinks he is doing. The decisive point is that he must always be setting himself in opposition to himself. There is no human existence without cleavage. Yet he cannot rest content in this cleavage. The way in which he overcomes it, the way in which he transcends it, reveals the conception he has of himself."[1]

KARL JASPERS

I

W. B. YEATS HAD A richer and more complex personality than either of the poets dealt with in the previous two chapters. In contradistinction to Thomas he did not live according to the dictates of instinct, but consciously and painfully shaped his life as he did his art, in order to invest it with the utmost degree of intensity and significance. He did not, like Whitman, strike a pose and reveal to the world but one aspect of himself and of the world he wrote about, but sought to reveal himself to himself and to his readers in all his various roles, and to contain all the diverse world of fact and experience within his system of thought and within his art.

Never was there more persistent a seeker after the unitive life, never a man more aware of the dichotomies within himself, than was William Butler Yeats. Believing that it is out of the quarrel with ourselves that poetry is made, he was ever holding up one aspect of his own complex character against another, and perpetually seeking to reconcile contrarieties and establish "unity of being" within himself.

It is doubtful whether he was ever wholly successful in this latter endeavour, but his writings, apart from their very great intrinsic poetic value, are interesting as a record of a spiritual life unique in its variety and intensity. He was the most restless of poets, the most impassioned seeker for a livable truth, which he believed would pull the diverse world together into a coherent whole. The dreamy minor poet of his early volumes became one of the very few heroic figures of our time. Indefatigably he pursued his personal truth, and as early as 1888 he could write in a letter to Katharine Tynan : "My life is in my poems. To make them I have broken my life in a mortar as it were."

But Yeats was not simply a dedicated artist ; many more figures have to be brought on the stage before we have anything resembling a picture of the whole man. The dreamy and introspective poet, the incorrigibly romantic Celt, the timid young man who hated London and longed for Sligo, the solitary who lived for the perfection of his art, are consistent with each other ; but on the other hand he appears at times in guises which are not so easily reconcilable, such as that of the energetic champion of Irish nationalism, the senator, the founder of the Abbey theatre, the dandified young art student and the young man who sat at Madame Blavatsky's feet and conducted his own experiments in magic. The impression we may at first get when considering the many apparently unrelated activities of Yeats's life is that he was a man without direction, unable to decide how and where to canalise his energies. This impression is far from the truth. All the activities that Yeats ever engaged in were embarked upon either as deliberate character-building expedients or in order to satisfy the needs of his deeper self. In youth he was abnormally sensitive and timid, but at the same time extremely strong-willed, and he forced himself into activities which were, to say the least, uncongenial for the poet in him. At that time he believed that a man's life should itself be a work of art. He admired the studied pose of Oscar Wilde and himself assumed attitudes towards the world which, if they were not consistent with his inner self, did give him a sense of mastery over life and compensate for his great uncertainty about himself. But even when he became older and more assured the poses remained. He had developed a theory, which became a central pillar of his thought, that all energy, all the creative drive in life, was generated by the tension caused by the conflict of opposites. Applying this to human character he concluded that intensity could only be maintained by the man who was able to assume the Mask of another life, the direct contrary of his own, of incarnating in himself his Anti-self : "If we cannot imagine ourselves as different from what we are, and try to assume that second self, we cannot impose a discipline upon ourselves though we may accept one from others." Only by imposing a discipline upon himself can man achieve anything in defiance of nature. The youthful Yeats slept on a board in order to make the images in his poetry more concrete and precise. The more mature poet laboured over his verses and with rigorous pen excised every word or image that seemed like an abstraction or was lacking in intensity. Some critics took him to task for his excessive conscientiousness, but he silenced them with four significant lines :

> "The friends that have it I do wrong
> Whenever I remake a song
> Should know what issue is at stake :
> It is myself that I remake."

Believing that "the self-conquest of the writer who is not a man of action is style", Yeats persistently worked at the task of forming a style which would be a fit vehicle for his "personal utterance." The result is that, more than in any other modern poet, the style is the man. In its development we have the key to the psychological development of the poet; the changes it undergoes are symptomatic of the changes in the poet's attitude to life.

But to speak of changes is to encourage the popular misconception that Yeats had a "butterfly mind" which flirted with one ideal or interpretation of life after another and never decided where to settle. A better word is "development", for Yeats's life and work developed consistently out of certain ideals which he arrived at in youth and maintained throughout his life. In his autobiography he expresses his conviction that "our intellects at twenty contain all the truths we shall ever find, but as yet we do not know truths that belong to us from opinions caught up in casual irritation or momentary fantasy." It was a conviction born of experience, and, whether or not it is of general validity, it is certainly true of Yeats himself. In his very earliest creative years he evolved his faith in the power of the human mind to control the universe, a faith which he found confirmed in his reading of Blake. This belief was the root cause of his interest in magic. The powers of the human imagination were unlimited, he believed, and in later life he went so far as to assert that by exercising these powers man had created the world, in fact that "man made up the whole/Made lock, stock and barrel/Out of his bitter soul." Also, when he was about twenty he told his father that truth was "the dramatically appropriate utterance of the highest man." It is not a very far cry from this to Kierkegaard's "truth is subjectivity" or to the magnificent declaration Yeats put into the mouth of Cuchulain in his last play : "I make the truth". Never did he lapse into mere dogmatism. Though his verse abounds in forceful assertions he never makes them otherwise than dramatically, whether in lyric or play ; so that their absolute truth is not in question, but only their dramatic appropriateness.

Yeats was profoundly and variously influenced by his father. From him he probably derived his belief in the poet as a man not committed to any consistent point of view, but a voice for the expression of all views and all emotions. John Butler Yeats wrote to his son that for the poet "the important thing is not that he keep his mental consistency but that he preserve the integrity of his soul." The preservation of the integrity of his soul, the conducting of life according to the "law of his own being" became one of the central objects of Yeats's life, and he never diverged from that law either for convenience or to make himself more consistent or comprehensible. But Yeats was far from being his father's disciple. The differences between the two were pronounced and their quarrels bitter. John Butler Yeats was a sceptic and a believer in science. His son, upholding the supremacy of the life of the imagination, revolted against science. In rebellion against his father's scepticism he sought confirmation of his belief in the supernatural life, and the search led him to Madame Blavatsky's feet and to participation in various groups pretending to esoteric wisdom. He was extraordinarily gullible, but even more extraordinary was his capacity for transmuting the dross of occult ideas into the purest gold of poetry. He derived many of his major symbols from his occult studies. Indeed the "unknown instructors," the spirits who dictated his wife's automatic writing and were thereby responsible for the book *A Vision*, declared that it was their purpose simply to give him metaphors for his poetry. A lesser poet, lacking an established tradition, would have been spoilt by dabbling in theosophy and occultism, but for Yeats poetry always came first. He was not seeking truths to incorporate in his poetry, but rather attempting to ascend to truth *through* his poetry. His supernatural studies had served their purpose when they had supplied him with symbols. He was not content, as were most of the other Symbolist poets who were his contemporaries, to evolve a personal system of symbols which would adequately express his experience and would constitute a closed-in world, but wished his symbols to have the authority of an existence distinct from his own, to be projected upon some external, established and unchanging reality as were those of poets living in an age of faith.

It was typical of Yeats to require external authority for his symbolism at a time when other poets were content both to exist and to create within the confines of their own selves. He was always aware of the imperfection and transience of human life, and a recurring theme in his writings is the celebration of the transcendent, especially when it appears in the form of a work of art, for in making such a work man became superman, confounding time and change by embodying externally the inner processes of his intellect or imagination. As he says in *Byzantium*:

> "A starlit or a moonlit dome disdains
>   All that man is,
>   All mere complexities,
>   The fury and the mire of human veins."

This is consistent with the Yeatsian principle that a thing becomes most completely itself when it has realised its opposite within itself. Inwardness transcends itself in being externalised.* Symbols gain in significance when they have some existence independent of the poet.

What saves Yeats from the intellectual flaccidity of most of the champions of occultism is his high ideal of the superhuman and his endeavour to attain to it himself by the discipline of his life and his art. It was his declared purpose "to condense as out of the flying vapour of the world an image of human perfection." For him perfection did not consist in moral virtue but in a life lived intensely and energetically, keeping consciousness at its highest pitch through the conflict of antinomies, and ultimately embodying the transcendent either in the dedicated life or in the perfect work of art.

II

Yeats ended his first volume of autobiography, *Reveries over Childhood and Youth*, with the words: "all life weighed

---

* That is, provided that the externalisation of such inwardness is a struggle to give it durable form and not a mere frittering away of its essence and energy. Nicolas Berdyaev believed that "externalisation of spirit" was one of the greatest dangers of our time, and Rilke's predominant belief was that the external world should be "transformed," "that its being may rise, again, 'invisibly', in us." On the surface it appears that the ideas of the two poets are directly contradictory. They are not so in fact. The same end is aimed at by both poets: the one by making the internal external, the other by making the external internal, seeks to effect transformation, to give permanence to the transitory and significance to what would otherwise be meaningless in its diffusion.

in the scales of my own life seems to me a preparation for something that never happens." His very last poem, *The Black Tower*, written a few days before his death, is about a band of men waiting in a besieged tower for a king who will never come to relieve them, though "the tower's old cook" —a symbol for the human imagination—sometimes thinks he hears the king's approach, but is always mistaken. It is significant that the theme of unfulfilled expectation should occur at two such crucial points in the poet's work. It is the key to the question we must now consider: that of Yeats's religious experience.

Yeats's life was indeed a waiting and a preparation for something which never transpired, and that something was a religious experience, a vision he called it, which would intitiate him into the world of Being, would give him a comprehensive view of life and an insight into its mysteries. From early youth he had admired Blake, but there was something within himself which, try as he may, he could never finally liberate, though if he had succeeded in doing so he felt that he would have assumed the terrible freedom and the visionary powers of his master. He never stopped disciplining himself and trying all natural ways he could contrive to stimulate his visionary faculties. Even in the posthumously published volume of his *Last Poems* we find him declaring:

> "Myself I must remake
> Till I am Timon and Lear
> Or that William Blake
> Who beat upon the wall
> Till Truth obeyed his call."

Yeats beat upon the wall with as much violence and perseverence as Blake or any other man, but Truth did not obey his call, and shortly before his death he wrote to a friend, saying, "When I try to put all into a phrase I say 'Man can embody truth but he cannot know it.'" Such was the final verdict of a man who had devoted his life to the quest for truth, and who went through a whole gamut of spiritual experience without being able to induce in himself the final condition of illuminative vision. Yeats never became a mystic in the sense that Blake was one, but nevertheless what he left us was something infinitely valuable : a record of the struggles, creative and stimulating in themselves, of a scrupulously honest human mind engaged in an heroic endeavour to know reality, and of those other struggles suffered by a representative modern man who would establish "Unity of Being" within himself in despite of the world.

Yeats went through the whole range of religious experience that we have described in the chapters on Thomas and Whitman, but without placing the emphasis as they did, for his attention was directed to a more distant goal, one difficult of attainment and requiring the determined exercise of his will and the concentration of his energy. He says in his autobiography that "in a species of man, wherein I count myself, nothing so much matters as Unity of Being . . . true Unity of Being, where all the nature murmurs in response if but a single note be touched, is found emotionally, instinctively, by the rejection of all experience not of the right quality, and by the limitation of its quantity." Elsewhere he goes further and suggests that such unity can only be established as a result of a crisis in life, when all a man's higher faculties are awakened and employed together to overcome that obstacle which is the greatest he may confront without despair. Such a crisis can be precipitated by a man assuming his Mask or Anti-self, by the dreamer becoming a man of action and the sensitive man experiencing violence :

> "Know that when all words are said
> And a man is fighting mad,
> Something drops from eyes long blind,
> He completes his partial mind,
> For an instant stands at ease,
> Laughs aloud, his heart at peace.

Even the wisest man grows tense
With some sort of violence
Before he can accomplish fate,
Know his work or choose his mate."

In order to "complete his partial mind" and realise Unity of Being, Yeats repeatedly forced moments of crisis upon himself, pitted one aspect of himself against another, or his whole self against some challenging aspect of the external world. And each of these struggles deepened his self knowledge. They also affected the style of his poetry, and in that changing style we can trace the various stages in the poet's spiritual development.

Readers who are more familiar with Yeats's early poetry than with his later will probably find it difficult to believe that in his daily life he was almost indifferent to the natural world. A friend remarked once how unobservant he was as far as natural phenomena were concerned. It was a true observation, for in Yeats's poetry the external world is present only as a sort of foil to the inner subjective world, so that the latter may most fully realise and express itself through its struggle with its opposite. In *Reveries Over Childhood and Youth* the poet tells how in his very early years "All my religious emotions were, I think, connected with clouds and cloudy glimpses of luminous sky." For a few years he studied natural life, read books and collected specimens, but in his teens he tired of it and "began to play at being a sage, a magician or a poet." Yeats was never a nature poet, and any natural imagery that appeared in his early work was an inheritance from the Romantic Movement rather than an expression of the poet's true self. Reviewing his work towards the end of his life in *The Circus Animal's Desertion* he said that these images "Grew in pure mind" and had their origin "In the foul rag-and-bone shop of the heart." Mind and heart, or spirit and flesh, are the twin springs which constitute the source of all that Yeats ever wrote. The whole man, and not merely the mind or the emotions, was involved in the writing of his poems, particularly the later ones, and it is to the whole man that they make their appeal. His is the poetry, not of nature, but of man, and his world is the world of the human spirit, both in its earthly and its transcendental manifestations. In 1934 he began *A Prayer for Old Age* with the lines.

> "God guard me from those thoughts men think
>   In the mind alone;
> He who sings a lasting song
>   Thinks in a marrow-bone."

In this, Yeats showed himself to be a genuine metaphysical poet, for that poetry is truly metaphysical which has its roots firmly established in the physical but is elevated beyond it by the impact of mind.

In Yeats's first three volumes, *Crossways* (1889), *The Rose* (1893), and *The Wind Among the Reeds* (1899), there is scarcely a hint of the major poet he was to become. These volumes are full of artifice, and everywhere the influence of the Pre-Raphaelites, whom he so admired in his youth, is evident. But even while he was writing them he was, in his poetic theory, moving away from such work. "I tried to write out of my emotions exactly as they came to me in life, not changing them to make them more beautiful" he said. But it was a long time before he began to think that those emotions themselves might be suspect, might not be profound at all, but mere romantic convention, and his poems a dramatisation of himself and his feelings. It was not until the twentieth century that he began to write out of his own experience of life, and not, as many young poets are prone to do, out of those emotions experienced vicariously in his reading. And it was probably Maude Gonne's unexpected marriage, for the poet a shattering emotional experience which he never forgot, that first brought the genuine and urgent personal note into his verse.

Yeats developed an interest in folk traditions quite early.

Ostensibly he turned to folk art in order to further the Nationalist cause, as a means of restoring to Ireland that Unity of Culture which modern nations had lost. But folk art meant more to him than this, for he saw in it the very antithesis of his own excessive self-consciousness. Moreover, it accepted the supernatural, in which the young poet had a firm but unreasoned faith, as a matter of course. He incorporated some of these traditions into his poetry, and in *The Wandering of Oisin* and his early plays attempted to re-create a folk art. The result was a curious mixture of the subjective and the objective, and the poet himself admitted that there were some things in *The Wanderings of Oisin* the significance of which only he could understand. The symbolism in his writings of this period certainly obscures the natural world, but it no more reveals the supernatural than do the stage tricks of flying on wires and appearing from behind the smoke produced by a small explosion. Yeats had yet to learn that the supernatural is not the denial but rather the sublimation of the natural. Though Blake had set him on the right track he had not yet discovered for himself and really understood the world of spirit.

In 1892 Yeats wrote to John O'Leary, "I have always considered myself a voice of what I believe to be a greater renaissance—the revolt of the soul against the intellect—now beginning in the world." At that time, and indeed for most of the succeeding decade, he considered that the intellect was "impure" and had no place in poetry. It was this, he realised later in life, that gave to so much of his early poetry the element of sentimentality which spoilt it. Slowly he was learning, developing, broadening his mind and soul, and in the first decade of the present century this process was speeded up as he became increasingly aware that intellect and imagination were not mutually exclusive categories, but rather complementary ones so far as poetry was concerned. The broad outlines of the stages in his personal and poetic development at this time can be traced in his occasional writings. In 1903 he wrote to Lady Gregory:

"You need not be troubled about my poetical faculty. I was never so full of new thoughts for verse though all thoughts quite unlike the old ones. My work has got far more masculine. It has more salt in it."

In a letter to George Russell written in 1904 he enlarged upon this, explaining the change his style had undergone:

"In my 'Land of Heart's Desire', and in some of my lyric verse of that time, there is an exaggeration of sentiment and sentimental beauty which I have come to think unmanly. . . . I have been fighting the prevalent decadence for years, and have but just got it under foot in my own heart—it is sentiment and sentimental sadness, a womanish introspection. . . . We possess nothing but the will and we must never let the children of vague desires breathe upon it nor the waters of sentiment rust the terrible mirror of its blade."

The emphasis has here shifted from the powers of the imagination to those of the will, the conscious and intellectually-controlled faculty. The poet is moving towards a positive religious attitude and away from his vague belief in the supernatural. In his poetry this reveals itself in a renewed endeavour to use the hard, precise, definite word. In 1905 he had written to John Quinn:

"I believe more strongly every day that the element of strength in poetic language is common idiom, just as the element of strength in poetic construction is common passion."

Two years later he felt he had made some positive progress in putting his theories into practise, for he wrote to Florence Farr:

"I at last find that I can move people by power, not merely—as the phrase is—by 'charm' or 'speaking beautifully'—a thing I always resented."

In the same year, 1907, he said in a letter to Lady Gregory:

> "I feel that I have lost myself—my centre as it were, has shifted from its natural interests, and that it will take me a long time finding myself again."

Though his poetic technique was now surer and more powerful, he still lacked the comprehensive view of life which would make his subject matter equally so. He was content, he said, with the "unruly soul" and with its moods as the subject matter of his poetry, but nevertheless he kept pressing forward, restlessly seeking a unified vision. In a diary entry made in 1909 he prayed:

> "O master of life give me confidence in something even if it be but my own reason."

But throughout his life he remained incapable of the humbling act of faith, being too conscious of human dignity and of the poet's high vocation. He could never either completely accept or reject Christianity. He felt that he had more in common with the pagan temperament of the Greeks, and declared:

> "Homer is my example and his unchristened art."

But the poem immediately before the one in which this line occurs ends with the question

> "What theme had Homer but original sin?"

He vacillates between paganism and Christianity, never reconciling them or making a choice between them, and indeed never really wishing to do so. Commitment to an established belief seemed to Yeats to involve the surrender of the thing he valued above all else: the life of the free imagination. He realised that "faith is the highest achievement of the human intellect, the only gift man can make to

God, and therefore it must be offered in sincerity", but he was not himself capable of holding a sincere faith, for his poetry drew the very sap of its existence from the conflict of opposites, and he feared lest the reconciliation of these in faith might cause the atrophy of his poetical faculties.

It was not a conscious decision of Yeats's not to commit himself to any faith, but rather the inevitable result of his being the man he was. He did, in fact, have the will to believe, and often longed for the assurance and repose which are the blessings of the faithful. At Rapallo in 1929 he made the following journal entry:

> "I must kill scepticism in myself, except in so far as it is mere acknowledgment of a limit. . . . The one reason for putting our actual situation into our art is that the struggle for complete affirmation may be, often must be, that art's chief poignancy. I must, though the world shriek at me, admit no act beyond my power, nor thing beyond my knowledge, yet because my divinity is far off I blanch and tremble."

This is a statement typical of the later Yeats, proud, courageous, defiant, yet aware of his limitations and intent upon changing himself. It is the awareness of a gap between the actual and the ideal that is the cause of all activity and progress in the spiritual sphere. Yeats had this awareness and he sought to bridge the gap, not as the saint does, by hollowing out his soul and making himself as nothing before God, but by so fulfilling himself by an act of will that he went beyond himself and attained to union with the ideal. Yeats tried to carry as much of himself into his God-relationship as possible, and he conceived that relationship as a struggle between God and man's promethean spirit. *The Four Ages of Man* may be considered as an autobiographical poem:

> "He with body waged a fight,
> But body won ; it walks upright.

Then he struggled with the heart;
Innocence and peace depart.

Then he struggled with the mind;
His proud heart he left behind.

Now his wars on God begin;
At stroke of midnight God shall win."

The "stroke of midnight" echoes through these later poems. Yeats would accept no religious dogmas about life after death, and consequently he was much possessed with the thought of his own age and that his spiritual pilgrimage seemed yet far from complete. In 1936 he underwent a rejuvenation operation, employing modern science in his war against God. He was determined not to give way until he had thoroughly explored his own soul and broken through "Into the desolation of reality." Right up to his death his poetry was, as always, a living thing. He never repeated himself, for there was always new experience to express, new thoughts to utter, and through discipline his verse had become a vehicle fit for the expression of all thoughts and all experiences. The style of his later poems, which appears so easy and natural, was the result of a lifetime's hard apprenticeship to the poetic craft. The language is terse and flexible, never vague or slovenly, the lines flow freely and naturally and the rhythms are strong though never monotonous. In short, he succeeded, in his later poems, in fulfilling his desire to think like a wise man but to express himself like the common people. The discipline of his verse which enabled him to achieve this was a reflection of the other discipline which he imposed upon his personal life and which was the cause of his ceaseless spiritual development.

It is a tribute to the monotheistic concept that a man like Yeats, beginning with a faith in occultism and spiritualism, should after a lifetime of development find the idea of a personal God the most profoundly satisfying. His God-relationship always remained one of struggle and conflict, but there are in the later poems occasions when God momentarily has the upper hand. In *The Statues* he denounces "All Asiatic vague immensities"—a thing he could never have done in the days when he was a disciple of Madame Blavatsky—and the last stanza of the Supernatural Song in which *Ribh Considers Christian Love Insufficient* is a direct statement of monotheistic faith :

"At stroke of midnight soul cannot endure
    A bodily or mental furniture.
    What can she take until her Master give !
    Where can she look until He make the show !
    What can she know until He bid her know !
    How can she live till in her blood He live !"

Yeats's straining after the more-than-human life, his efforts to shake free in himself a vision comparable to that of Blake, carried him to the very heights of the possible within the human sphere. He never became a saint or mystic, and though he may sometimes have considered this to be his failure, it is in fact a condition of the individuality of his poetry and his personality. "We have nothing but the will" he declared in the letter to George Russell which I have quoted, and by the exercise of his will he succeeded in raising himself, at least in the moments of creation, from the human to the superhuman plane without ever passing over into the divine and thus losing touch with common experience. He was, always, essentially human, and for that reason he strikes us as being heroic, for his life epitomises the eternal striving of man to transcend himself in spite of his being eternally frustrated by the fact of his mortality. Heroism does not consist only in courageous action on the field of battle : the existential hero is he who dares to face himself. Yeats did this with a fearful honesty ; and though he may have worn a mask before the world, before his own eyes his soul was stripped bare and mercilessly analysed. The truly heroic figure expresses the pathos as well as the nobility of human existence ; fully conscious of his own mortality and of the impermanence of the world, he yet wins through to affirmation. The saint and the mystic having transcended the world of becoming, which is that of human life, automatically cast the pathetic from themselves, and therefore are not heroic.

The saint and the mystic may conceivably ascend to the Absolute Truth, but for the normal human being there is no chance of his winning such eternal assurance during his mortal lifetime, though he may glimpse it occasionally. No man has ever sought to know Truth more persistently than did W. B. Yeats, and no man has failed more magnificently. But, on second thoughts, did he fail? Did he not, after all, succeed in realising himself, though that self was different from Blake whom he would have liked to emulate? At the end of his life his own thoughts turned in this direction and he wrote in one of his last letters:

"It seems to me that I have found what I wanted. When I try to put all into a phrase I say 'Man can embody truth but he cannot know it.' I must embody it in the completion of my life. The abstract is not life and everywhere drags out its contradictions. You can refute Hegel but not the Saint or the Song of Sixpence."

The Saint and the Song of Sixpence—action and art—cannot be refuted. Only the man who acts—and who seeks through action either to know or to express himself—and he who creates, can know reality. A lifetime devoted to abstract thought advances man no more than an afternoon at a football match. Such a handful of truths were the fruit of the experience of a lifetime. But it is not the truths that matter, but the living experience itself as it is set down for all time in those perfectly wrought poems, which are at once a monument to their author's heroic dedication to his task and a tribute to the human spirit, which is capable of transcending the ephemeral body to which it is bound.

E

III

Yeats is the first of the poets we have so far considered who acknowledged the importance of the life of the intellect and who was concerned with metaphysical issues. When using this latter term it is of supreme importance that we should distinguish between the metaphysics which explores in a leisurely way the problems of the nature of Truth, the nature of Reality and the nature of Being, and that other metaphysics which, arising out of human need in particular situations, *feels* these problems to be closely connected with actual life. Yeats was not an armchair metaphysician, he was an existential thinker, that is to say he was a man whose concern it was to create for himself by means of thought an existence which should be meaningful and truly human. This he did, as do all such thinkers, by conceiving an ideal and by bending all his faculties, physical as well as intellectual, to the task of realising it. His ideal was the superhuman.

> "I hail the superhuman ;
> I call it death-in-life and life-in-death."

Here the fundamental problem is stated : the superhuman is also anti-human, for it is not compatible with life-in-the-world. The relationship between the human and the super-human, the ideal and the actual, the sensual and the spiritual, the inner life and the external life, became the central problem of Yeats's thought. On occasions he was inclined to renounce the world completely, and prayed to be "gathered into the artifice of eternity", but at other times he was content to "choose the second best" and "forget it all awhile/ Upon a woman's breast". Life was, to his mind, a condition of dynamic tension between opposites, and the releasing of that tension would constitute a denial of human life. His function as a poet was not to be consistent, but to be passionate, for only with passion can any view of life, or life itself be affirmed. But passion does not reconcile, and on the human plane there can be no reconciliation of the conflicting opposites. The man who wishes to remain a poet cannot sever himself from the human, however strong may be his inclination towards the divine or the superhuman, for poetry is movement, and, as Blake said, "without contraries is no progression". So the poet is forced to make a choice between the two alternatives propounded by Kierkegaard in his *Either/Or* : either the aesthetic life or the ethico-religious life. Yeats expressed the dilemma in a poem called *The Choice* :

> "The intellect of man is forced to choose
> Perfection of the life, or of the work,
> And if it take the second must refuse
> A heavenly mansion, raging in the dark."

Yeats never actually made the choice which he thought necessary, though his indecision meant that ultimately he settled for the aesthetic life, for perfection of the work. But the ethico-religious life continued to draw him, though he could not commit himself to it because such commitment seemed to involve a renunciation of the world of the senses, a passing beyond human passion. So he vacillated between the two alternatives. In fact he wrote a group of poems under the title *Vacillation*, the seventh of which sums up his dilemma and his implied choice in six lines :

> "*The Soul*. Seek out reality, leave things that seem.
> *The Heart*. What, be a singer born and lack a theme?
> *The Soul*. Isaiah's coal, what more can man desire?
> *The Heart*. Struck dumb in the simplicity of fire!
> *The Soul*. Look on that fire, salvation walks within.
> *The Heart*. What theme had Homer but original sin?"

It is for the saint to "seek out reality," for the poet is bound by his senses and by his humanity to the world of appearances. The reference in the third line is to the burning coal with which one of the seraphims touched Isaiah's lips, saying, "thine iniquity is taken away, and thy sin purged."[2] The poet does not wish to have his iniquity taken away, and he will choose to forego salvation that he may take man's original sin as his theme.

Feeling himself cut off from the saint's way by his poetic vocation, Yeats sought other means of attaining to the state of unitive vision. He remembered the example of Dante, who, in the words of Boccacio, "Always, both in youth and maturity, found room among his virtues for lechery." Of Dante he wrote in *Ego Dominus Tuus* that

> "Being mocked by Guido for his lecherous life,
> Derided and deriding, driven out
> To climb that stair and eat that bitter bread,
> He found the unpersuadable justice, he found
> The most exalted lady loved by a man."

It was the Image of Beatrice that enabled Dante, though he was a sensualist and a man of the world, to experience his vision. Might not Yeats also find such an Image which would carry him beyond himself? Might he not force a crisis by confronting the Image of his anti-self, and thus gain access to the depths of his own being? "Revelation," he had now learnt, "is from the self, but from that age-long memoried self, that shapes the elaborate shell of the mollusc and the child in the womb, that teaches the birds to make their nest; and genius is a crisis that joins that buried self for certain moments to our trivial daily mind." The exalted Image of Beatrice had enabled Dante, through passion, to keep his buried self before his conscious mind, and thus to sustain the state of illuminative vision. Yeats never discovered an Image capable of doing this for him and consequently his poetry is a series of brilliant moments, moments of wilfully induced intensity, which marvellously mirror existence but do not resolve it.

Yeats was urged by the deepest instincts of his being to pursue the unitive life, but the attachment of the poet to the contingent world forbade him the experience of union with the Absolute. Nevertheless, he always tried to attain in his thought to that comprehensive view of the world which he

imagined such an experience would have given him. He saw
clearly that man was divided into many parts, that he warred
incessantly with himself, but he saw also the mysterious
union beyond this division, saw that there was no part but
had reference to the whole. His function as a poet was to
affirm, and to affirm the whole, however difficult that may
be. In fact it was precisely because it was difficult that it was
essential to affirm, and to affirm with passion, for only the
most difficult of tasks causes a man to exercise his faculties
to the fullest. In *Per Amica Silentia Lunae* Yeats wrote: "We
must not create, by hiding ugliness, a false beauty as our
offering to the world. He only can create the greatest imaginable beauty who has endured all imaginable pangs, for
only when we have seen and foreseen what we dread shall
we be rewarded by that dazzling unforeseen wing-footed
wanderer." Here is a high ideal which the poet himself tried
to live up to. No experience was too bitter for him, no fact
too terrible. All facts and all experiences were patiently
and painfully assimilated by him, and, like the heroes of
Easter 1916, were

> "All changed, changed utterly:
> A terrible beauty is born."

The terrible beauty that was born of this process of catholic
assimilation was that of the art of the uncompromising
realist, and Yeats, by his unwillingness to make any rejec-
tions, revealed himself as a truly modern man and one of the
greatest realistic poets of our or any age.

It was partly this unwillingness to reject any part of the
whole which is man and his world that kept Yeats clear of
institutional religions and their dogmatic systems of
thought. In one of his last poems, *News for the Delphic
Oracle*, he presents three different pictures of heaven. The
first is the Greek pagan ideal, over-refined and passionless,
the second is a Christian heaven where men are relieved of
their burdens, and the third a creation of the Yeatsian
imagination, a heaven which satisfies the whole man, where

"nymphs and satyrs/Copulate in the foam", and the functions of the body and those of the spirit are not mutually exclusive. Religions which denied or ignored man's physical being were anathema to Yeats, for whom religion was nothing if not the act of affirming the existential. In the story of *The Three Bushes*, which also appeared in *Last Poems*, the same idea is symbolically stated. The lady who loved with her soul and the chambermaid whom she sent in her stead to her lover's bed both loved equally though neither loved completely, for the love of the body and the soul's love are complementary and not opposed to each other. It would be impossible to make sense of the world if the Mediaeval Christian theologians were right in their belief that spirit and matter were irreconcilably in opposition. The two were obviously indivisible and interdependent. In the last stanza of *Among School Children* Yeats posed, beautifully if a little enigmatically, the metaphysical question :

"Labour is blossoming or dancing where
The body is not bruised to pleasure soul,
Nor beauty born out of its own despair,
Nor blear-eyed wisdom out of midnight oil.
O chestnut tree, great-rooted blossomer,
Are you the leaf, the blossom or the bole?
O body swayed to music, O brightening glance,
How can we know the dancer from the dance?"

Can the essential nature of a chestnut-tree be located in any of its parts? Can a beautiful dance have an existence independent of the dancer? Can the spiritual manifest itself otherwise than through the material? Yeats answered these questions with a categorical negative, and he proceeded to seek, beyond Christianity, for a personal faith which would equally affirm the material and the physical aspects of human existence, and not subordinate them to the spiritual. In his later poems he became increasingly preoccupied with sex, partly out of defiance and partly because he came to regard

sex symbolically as a process wherein the physical simultaneously fulfils itself and surpasses itself, passing over into
a condition of serenity which is beyond division and strife.

Affirmation was made the more difficult for Yeats by the
fact that, unlike either Thomas or Whitman, he had an
acute Vision of Evil. Moreover, he understood the importance of this to the artist, realised that it was when his Vision
of Evil was intense that a man could bring his life to crisis
and immeasurably deepen thereby his grasp of reality. In
his autobiography he wrote: "Had not Dante and Villon
understood that their fate wrecked what life could not
rebuild, had they lacked their Vision of Evil, had they
cherished any species of optimism, they could but have
found a false beauty, or some momentary instinctive beauty,
and suffered no change at all. . . ." The despair and the
suffering which the Vision of Evil brings in its wake are
purgative experiences without which no life may become
truly human. He who has suffered much and most deeply
despaired, and yet affirms, is of all men the most profoundly
human and the most heroic. In early manhood Yeats
suffered greatly from his frustrated love for Maude Gonne,
and in maturity from the thought that he was ageing but
apparently approaching no nearer to his vision. Age irritated
him, and it is doubtful whether any poet has revolted so
vehemently against growing old and so bitterly scorned
the "body and its stupidity." In *Sailing to Byzantium* he
declared:

> "An aged man is but a paltry thing,
>   A tattered coat upon a stick, unless
>   Soul clap its hands and sing, and louder sing
> For every tatter in its mortal dress."

To the very end Yeats's soul clapped its hands and sang in
defiance of old age and mortality. In *The Man and the Echo*—
one of the last poems he wrote—his most powerful statement
of affirmation arises directly out of a mood of despair:

Man

"All that I have said and done,
Now that I am old and ill,
Turns into a question till
I lay awake night after night
And never get the answers right.

. . . . .

And all seems evil until I
Sleepless would lie down and die.

Echo

Lie down and die.

Man

That were to shirk
The spiritual intellect's great work,
And shirk it in vain. There is no release
In a bodkin or disease,
Nor can there be work so great
As that which cleans man's dirty slate.
While man can still his body keep
Wine or love drug him to sleep,
Waking he thanks the Lord that he
Has body and its stupidity,
But body gone he sleeps no more,
And till his intellect grows sure
That all's arranged in one clear view,
Pursues the thoughts that I pursue,
Then stands in judgment on his soul,
And, all work done, dismisses all
Out of intellect and sight
And sinks at last into the night."

If Yeats failed in his desire to see "all arranged in one clear view" he made out of his failure lasting poetry, poetry which future generations may come to regard as one of the highest achievements of the human spirit; for in an age when the stature of man had been reduced it dared to celebrate the superhuman, and for all time it will represent the power man has to triumph over himself and over his fate.

CHAPTER FOUR

ANGEL AND DEMON: A STUDY OF ARTHUR RIMBAUD

"When a man is in one of these two states, it is well with him, and he can be as safe in hell as in heaven, and so long as a man is on earth, it is possible for him to pass ofttimes from the one to the other. . . . But when a man is in neither of these two, he holds converse with the creature, and wavers hither and thither, and knows not where he is. Therefore let him never forget either of them in his heart."[1]

Theologia Germanica

BAUDELAIRE DIED IN 1867, three years before Arthur Rimbaud, after walking off with all the school prizes in his native town of Charleville, made his first gesture of revolt by forsaking his home, his family, his promising academic future, and embarking upon his brief, but tempestuous and dazzling, literary career. That was in 1870, when Rimbaud was sixteen years old, and that career lasted approximately until the end of 1874. Those four years saw the production by the Ardennais peasant boy of some of the purest poetry and most searching self analysis that the student of literature or of man will find in any language. But I am forgetting Baudelaire. This chapter began with his name because for Rimbaud Baudelaire was "le premier voyant, roi des poètes, *un vrai Dieu*";* and it is hardly possible to over-emphasise the profound influence which the elder poet had upon the younger. In a passage in *Mon Cœur mis à nu* Baudelaire wrote of the particular dichotomy which is the key to Rimbaud's spiritual biography:

"Il y a dans tout homme, à toute heure, deux postulations simultanées, l'une vers Dieu, l'autre vers Satan.

* "the first visionary, the king of poets, a real God."

L'invocation à Dieu, ou spiritualité, est un désir de monter en grade ; celle de Satan, ou animalité, est une joie de descendre."

"There are in every man, always, two simultaneous allegiances, one to God, the other to Satan. Invocation of God, or Spirituality, is a desire to climb higher; that of Satan, or animality, is delight in descent."[2]

In all that he ever undertook Rimbaud was an extremist, an absolutist. He put all the fervour of his passionate and energetic being into the attempt to experience the highest peak of exaltation and the deepest abyss of degradation possible for man. He transcended the human sphere in both directions : in his soarings to heaven he became an angel, in his descents into hell he became a demon and beast.

It is possible to read a great deal into Rimbaud's life and writings, to find there support for almost any position or belief. Of the thirty-seven years of Rimbaud's life five were spent on creative literary work, but in that time he passed through a veritable Odyssey of spiritual experience, such as few men are privileged, or rather fated, to undergo, even during the span of a normal lifetime. He developed rapidly and restlessly, and at the same time his command of language developed, so that he was always able to give expression to his experience. In some of the *Illuminations* that expression is elliptical and densely symbolical, and a sympathetic sensibility and a quick imagination are required of the reader who seeks truly to understand them. This very elusiveness has resulted in much of Rimbaud being misread and enlisted in support of some theory which would never have entered his head. Critics have seen him as a Catholic and as a pagan, a mystic and a Marxist, as the father of Surrealism and the spiritual descendant of the Hebrew Prophets, as God incarnate and as the Devil in human form, as an Angel, a being free from original sin, and as Prometheus, the fire-stealer. Perhaps all these ideas are partial truths, but they do not add up to make a whole man. Interpretation may be protracted over the years and throughout a thousand volumes, but the works of the boy poet will remain, in their purity and freedom from conceptual thought, a lasting monument to the central mystery of life, the mystery of creation.

The example of Rimbaud carries my thesis forward because, like Yeats, he consciously and deliberately sought to change his life. By an act of will he tried to force himself into a vision of reality, and he succeeded in reaching that stage where the will is suspended and the vision reveals itself. In other words, he was a true mystic. The complete liberation for which Yeats's deepest being yearned could only have been brought about by a suspension of his own will and an absolute dedication to the task of knowing reality, at no matter what cost to himself. But Yeats clung to poetry, whereas Rimbaud, when he found that poetry could carry him no further along the road to the apprehension of the ultimately real, abandoned it without hesitation. This may be regretted, for he was a man of impeccable artistic gifts, but he was ruled by the inflexible temperament of the mystic, and in so far as the limits of art are the limits of the human, he transcended them.

Nietzsche, though he was his contemporary, never knew about the French boy who came so close to incarnating his concept of the Superman. The many similarities between the two need not be investigated here; it is sufficient for our purpose to note how the poetic theory of Nietzsche underlines the practice of Rimbaud. The German philosopher believed that two basic elements contribute to the creation of a work of art, one of which he called the Apollonian, and the other the Dionysian, element. The former is the impulse towards harmony and perfection, the latter the pull towards chaos. In Rimbaud's work both can be seen in operation. Some of the *Illuminations* are purely Apollonian, whereas *Une Saison en Enfer* is one of the finest examples of Dionysian literature to be found anywhere. Rimbaud's Vision of Evil was more penetrating even than that of Yeats. Evil was for him a metaphysical reality which he had deeply experienced and explored. But though the inclination towards evil was stronger in him than in most men, to speak of him as a sinner would be a mistake. The only sin of which he may be considered guilty is that of spiritual pride. It was this pride which made him suppose he could stand alone in the universe as God's equal, autonomous and perpetually creative in his solitude—a supposition which is in part justified by the divine creative power which flowed from him into the composition of the *Illuminations*. But though he was intent on experiencing evil in all its various manifestations—hence his addiction to drugs and alcohol, his homosexuality and his sadism—he never sinned, for he had no joy in these indulgences. He was a kind of inverted ascetic seeking purification through experience of evil. His later behaviour in Abyssinia, when he managed to save a considerable sum of money out of a meagre income, testifies to the naturally abstemious and ascetic nature of his way of life. And perhaps the very fact of his being drawn to such an arid part of the world has its psychological explanation. The predominant impulse in both his life and his work was a yearning for absolute purity. In the *Illuminations* he attained to a purity of style unknown in French literature since Racine—whom he admired second only to Baudelaire. At the end of *L'Impossible* in *Une Saison en Enfer* he wrote ecstatically:

> "O pureté ! pureté !
> "C'est cette minute d'éveil qui m'a donné la vision de la pureté !—Par l'esprit on va à Dieu !"

> "O purity, purity !
> "This moment of wakefulness has given me the vision of purity !—The mind leads one to God !"[3]

Rimbaud longed always for an existence of purer spirituality. He was never content with the limitations of human life, which he constantly sought to transcend. His descent into hell was just such an act of transcendence. It was the converse of the saint's self denial, though its object was the same, namely, purification. The fires of hell purge man of mediocrity, of slothfulness ; and the deliberate embracing of evil is an act to which he applies all the intensity of his being. That is why the author of the *Theologia Germanica*, in the passage quoted as the epigraph to this chapter, says that when a man is neither in heaven nor hell he "wavers hither and thither, and knows not where he is." There was no wavering in Rimbaud's life, he flung himself uncompromisingly into everything he embarked upon. His descent into hell was an attempt to discover the Absolute Hell, the very rock-bottom of degradation. He failed in this because he could never completely extinguish the divine fire within himself. Innocence and purity remained the cornerstones of his character in the midst of the most extreme of his excesses, and he succeeded in spending only a brief *Season in Hell*.

In his essay *Le Secret Professionel* Jean Cocteau has the following sentence :

"Jusqu'à nouvel ordre, Arthur Rimbaud reste le type de l'ange sur terre."[4]

"Until further notice, Arthur Rimbaud remains the type of the angel on earth."

The concept suits him, for Rimbaud was angelic not only by reason of his endemic purity and innocence, but also because his apprehension of the infinite was so strong that the conditions of finite human life were insupportable for him. "La vraie vie est absente"* he declared, and "l'amour est a réinventer."† No human relationship could fully satisfy him. The love of women fell far short of his ideal of "un amour multiple et complexe ! . . . un bonheur indicible, insupportable même !"‡[5] The most important relationship of his life —that with Paul Verlaine which ended dramatically after two years with the latter shooting Rimbaud in the wrist in a Brussels hotel—failed to fulfil the promise which the

* "True life is not here" (*Une Saison en Enfer*).

† "love must be re-invented" (*Une Saison en Enfer*).

‡ "a rich and complex love . . . an indescribable, unbearable happiness" (*Les Illuminations, Conte*).

younger poet had at first seen in it. Verlaine was too weak-minded, pietistic and spiritually sluggish to understand the ecstasies and despairs of his young friend. "S'il m'expliquait ses tristesses, les comprendrais-je plus que ses railleries?"* Rimbaud makes him say in the first of the two *Délires* in *Une Saison en Enfer*, where Verlaine is depicted as the Foolish Virgin and himself as the Infernal Husband. Verlaine did not understand that what was for him as indulgence of his weakness was for Rimbaud a stage in his spiritual development, the stage of purification. The two men were temperamentally very different, and though for a time the relationship fulfilled both their needs, it was too intense to be lasting. The *Illumination* called *Vagabonds* provides a key to the nature of the relationship. Its last paragraph reads:

"J'avais en effet, en toute sincérité d'esprit, pris l'engagement de le rendre à son état primitif de fils du Soleil,—et nous errions, nourris du vin des cavernes et du biscuit de la route, moi pressé de trouver le lieu et la formule."

"In deepest sincerity, I had pledged to convert him back into his primitive state of a Sun-god,—and we wandered, sustained by wine from caverns and a traveller's crust, with me impatient to find the place and the formula."

In endeavouring to restore him to his primitive state of a Sun-god Rimbaud was applying to his friend his own standard of what a poet should be, a standard derived from his own experience and achievement, and inapplicable to a man of so different a temperament as Paul Verlaine. He seems to have realised this, for the last line, "moi pressé de trouver le lieu et la formule", pictures Rimbaud as he always was, a solitary and indefatigable seeker for the golden key to life's mysteries.

* "If he explained his sorrows to me, would I understand them any better than his mockery?" (*Une Saison en Enfer*).

In the *Illumination* called *Conte* Rimbaud expressed symbolically much of his own spiritual experience. *Conte* is the story of a prince who, dissatisfied with his wives, his followers, his pet animals and his palaces, destroys them all, hoping to attain to self knowledge in the very act of destruction. In the question "Peut-on s'extasier dans la destruction, se rajeunir par la cruaté !"* we hear the voice of Rimbaud himself, asking a question about which he was long in doubt. But even more important than these for the light they cast on the poet's character are the lines in the first paragraph where he says of the Prince :

> 'Il prévoyait d'étonnantes révolutions de l'amour, et soupçonnait ses femmes de pouvoir mieux que cette complaisance agrémentée de ciel et de luxe. Il voulait voir la vérité, l'heure du désir et de la satisfaction essentiels. Que ce fût ou non une aberration de piété, il voulut. Il possédait au moins un assez large pouvoir humain."

> "He could foretell amazing revolutions of love, and suspected his wives of being able to give him more than their complacency, enhanced with ideals and wealth. He wanted to see truth and the time of full desire and satisfaction. He wanted this, even if it was a misuse of piety. At least he possessed a large reserve of human power."

In Rimbaud there was the same dissatisfaction with anything that another human being could give him, the same intuition of a something better, the same desire to see truth, and, above all, it could be said of him as of very few of his contemporaries that he possessed "un assez large pouvoir humain."

But Rimbaud was not content to have a large reserve of human power. He wanted divine power, the power to create out of nothing and to be able by an act of will to destroy whatever he or anyone else had created. He had read much

---

* "Can man reach ecstasy in destruction and be rejuvenated by cruelty?"

of Éliphas Lévi and other writers on magic, occultism and hermetic philosophy, and was profoundly influenced by them. Again the resemblance to Yeats is notable, and both poets were attracted to magic for the same reason, namely because they wished *consciously to change their lives*. "Il a peut-être des secrets pour *changer la vie*?"* asks the Verlaine figure in *Une Saison en Enfer*, and goes on to reply, "Non, il ne fait qu'en chercher."† The ways in which he sought to change his life were several, but they can be considered under two categories. Indeed, Rimbaud himself so divided them when he wrote the two *Délires* in *Une Saison en Enfer*. Firstly he tried to effect the change through the power of his will, and secondly through the power of language.

It was by the power of his will that Rimbaud embraced the life of debauchery, the life which was for him a martyrdom because it was so contrary to his essential nature. But this was but one aspect of a larger scale operation by which he sought to pass beyond the boundaries of the material world and arrive at the unknown. He had read of the mediaeval alchemists, who sought to transmute base metal into gold by a process which began with the breaking down of the metal into its component parts, parts which, after purification and distillation, were combined together in a new unity which, if the operation were successful, would be gold. Rimbaud's ambition was to discover the pure gold of the spiritual life, to transmute base human life into pure spirituality, and in the way he set about doing this the correspondence with the alchemical process is evident. The three stages of disintegration, purification and unification follow each other in his theory as in that of the hermetic philosophers. It was in the so-called *Lettre du Voyant*, which he wrote to his friend Paul Demeny in May 1871, that Rimbaud most fully expressed his poetic theory. In Rimbaud, poetic theory and his ideas about the cultivation of the spiritual life are inseparable, for, as we have already noted, poetry was for him a means of apprehending the Absolute. It was in this

* "Perhaps he had secrets for *transforming life*."
† "No, he is only looking for them."

letter that Rimbaud wrote his famous sentence about the
"derangement of the senses"—the process which corresponds, of course, to the initial stage in the alchemical process, the stage of disintegration. Here is the passage from
the *Lettre du Voyant*:

"Le Poète se fait *voyant* par un long, immense et
raisonné *dérèglement de tous les sens*. Toutes le formes
d'amour, de souffrance, de folie ; il cherche lui-même, il
épuise en lui tous les poisons, pour n'en garder que les
quintessences. Ineffable torture où il a besoin de toute la
foi, de toute la force surhumaine, où il devient entre tous
le grand malade, le grand criminel, le grand maudit,—et
le suprême Savant !—car il arrive à l'*inconnu* !"

"The poet makes himself a visionary by a long,
immense and reasoned *derangement of all the senses*. All the
forms of love, of suffering and of madness ; he searches
himself, he drains all poisons from himself, in order to
keep only their quintessences. Unspeakable torture in
which he needs all his faith, all his superhuman power,
by which he becomes above all others the great sufferer,
the great criminal, the great outcast—and the supreme
Knower !—for he arrives at *the unknown*."

The influence of Baudelaire is evident here, and indeed
the terms "le grand malade, le grand criminel, le grand
maudit" are applicable to him as to no other poet. But
Rimbaud would have hesitated about applying the term "le
suprême Savant" to Baudelaire, for he believed that the
latter poet had not gone far enough, that he had been content with self knowledge and had not sought to know *the
unknown*. He had not, in other words, attempted to penetrate those regions beyond the world which are accessible
only to the mystic, and of the existence of which the mystical
temperament alone is aware. Rimbaud was a mystic, was
continually soaring beyond the world, and consequently his
criticism of Baudelaire is founded upon such criteria as only

give it a limited validity. When Rimbaud the poet, as distinct from Rimbaud the mystic, confronted Baudelaire, he
was unreserved in his praise. It is doubtful whether Rimbaud knew much about the details of his predecessor's life,
because Baudelaire's letters to his mother were not published
until some time after the boy's literary career was over.
However, there is a notable similarity between the two
poets in that they both resorted to artificial means of stimulating their imaginative and visionary faculties. Rimbaud's
period of drug-addiction was comparatively short, but he
had other means of deranging his senses, such as sacrificing
food and sleep and indulging his baser instincts. By such
means he cultivated in himself the habit of hallucination :

"Je m'habituai à l'hallucination simple : je voyais très
franchement une mosquée à la place d'une usine, une
école de tambours faite par des anges, des calèches sur les
routes du ciel, un salon au fond d'un lac ; les monstres,
les mystères ; un titre de vaudeville dressait des épou-
vantes devant moi" (*Une Saison en Enfer*).

"I accustomed myself to simple hallucination : I really
saw a mosque in place of a factory, angels practising on
drums, coaches on the roads across the sky ; a drawing-
room at the bottom of a lake : monsters, mysteries. The
title of a musical comedy could raise up terrors before
me."

Thus Rimbaud employed the powers of his will in order
to "changer la vie". To the same end also he used the
powers of language, powers which, he believed, had been in
abeyance since language became more concerned with the
expression of conceptual thought than of feelings and
intuitions. In one of his earliest poems, *Soleil et Chair*,
occurs the line :

"Notre pâle raison nous cache l'infini ;"*

* "Our pale reason hides the infinite from us."

and from that time onwards he lost no opportunity of stress-
ing the fact that mere reason, and the logical, discursive
means of expression which it employs, are hopelessly inadequate for the man who wishes to apprehend the infinite or
the Absolute. In *Une Saison en Enfer* he addressed Satan as
"vous qui aimez dans l'écrivain l'absence des facultés des-
criptives ou instructives."* As he conceived it, the function
of the poet was neither to describe nor to teach, but to
extend the boundaries of the expressible to those feelings
and intuitions which in most lives, if they are experienced at
all, pass unrecorded. The *Illuminations* are a series of such
moments of illuminated insight. "Insight", however, is a
misleading word to use in this connection, for it suggests
that these moments, which are moments of pure experience,
must have some dogmatic or moral content. The *Illuminations* are difficult reading for some people precisely because
they lack this. They will not yield themselves to rational
interpretation, and he who seeks ideas or "truths" in them
will find them meaningless. They are simply moments such
as those of which Martin Buber speaks when he says, in *I
And Thou* that :

> "There are moments of silent depth in which you look
> on the world-order fully present. Then in its very flight
> the note will be heard ; but the ordered world is its indis-
> tinguishable score. These moments are immortal, and
> most transitory of all ; no content may be secured from
> them, but their power invades creation and the know-
> ledge of man, beams of their power stream into the
> ordered world and dissolve it again and again."[6]

Rimbaud not only used language, he forged it. He sought
to strip from the word the encrustations of centuries of use
and restore the direct relationship between the word and the
emotional experience. It was his ambition to "inventer un
verbe poétique accessible, un jour au l'autre, à tous les

---

* "you who love in a writer the absence of descriptive or instructive
talent."

sens."* For him words were magical, were means by which he could "arrivcr a l'inconnu". He claimed, and with some justification, that in his poetic writings he had crossed frontiers never previously explored :

"J'écrivais des silences, des nuits, je notais l'inexprim-able. Je fixais des vertiges."

"I wrote of silences, of nights, I annotated the inex-pressible. I arrested moments of vertigo."

In his poetic theory as well as in his life Rimbaud was guilty of the sin of *hubris*, of over-reaching himself. As he himself realised, he reached the point where the disorder of his mind became sacred to him ("Je finis par trouver sacré le désordre de mon esprit"†). He resorted too often and too absolutely to artificial and violent means of inducing the visionary state, with the result that he experienced not visions but hallucinations, perceived not the ultimate reality but a series of unreal and fantastic images. In a lucid moment quite early in his career—when he wrote *Le Bateau Ivre*—he had foreseen that the exaltation occasioned by his attempts to "changer la vie" would be followed by disillu-sion when he discovered that it was not through violent experiences that he could apprehend "la vraie vie", but that he required for the purpose qualities which he never possessed, namely patience and a capacity for working without immediate reward. Rimbaud wanted quick results and his proud nature would not allow him to work patiently towards an end. He was too conscious of his elect position to follow any common path of achievement or to submit him-self to the laws which normally govern human life. He believed himself to be exempt from such laws by reason of his divine power as a creator. His acquaintance with writings on the subject of magic had caused him to believe in the

* "invent a poetic terminology that would one day be accessible to all the senses" (*Une Saison en Enfer*).

† "I ended up by regarding my mental disorder as sacred" (op. cit.)

existence of laws superior to the laws of nature, and he imagined that he was himself an Adept with abnormal powers. Not only did he have the power to conduct his own life according to its own law, but he believed that he was capable of inventing new flowers, new colours, new languages and new worlds. There is a passage in *Nuit de l'Enfer* where he speaks frankly of the powers he believes himself to possess:

"Je vais dévoiler tous les mystères : mystères religieux ou naturels, mort, naissance, avenir, passé, cosmogonie, néant. Je suis maître en fantasmagories.

"Écoutez ! . . .

"J'ai tous les talents !—Il n'y a personne ici et il y a quelqu'un : je ne voudrais pas répandre mon trésor.— Veut-on des chants nègres, des danses de houris ? Veut-on que je disparaisse, que je plonge à la recherche de l'*anneau* ? Veut-on ? Je ferai de l'or, des remèdes."

"I am about to unveil all mysteries: mysteries religious or natural, death, birth, future, past, the cosmogony, the void. I am a master of phantasmagoria.

"Listen ! . . .

"I have all the talents ! There is nobody here, yet there is somebody. I do not care to squander my treasure. Would you like negro songs, or houri dances? Would you like me to disappear, or to dive in search of *the ring*? Would you like that? I will make gold, or remedies."

Such promethean confidence in his own powers was bound to lead eventually to disillusionment. The law of *hubris*, as the Greeks discovered, is omnipotent, and in Christian mythology the example of Lucifer shows that not even the angels are exempt from it. Angel or man, Arthur Rimbaud certainly was not exempt, and he suffered deeply when he discovered that, for all his ambitions, he was no more initiated into the great mysteries of life than were the literary men whom he scorned.

It is curious how exactly the voyage of the Drunken Boat, in the poem written so early in his career, parallels and anticipates the progress of Rimbaud's own religious life. The Drunken Boat was an apt symbol for the poet's inner self, which journeyed over uncharted regions of spiritual experience and endeavoured to sound the unfathomable depths of its mysteries. A brief analysis of the poem will contribute to our understanding of its author.

In the first stanzas of *Le Bateau Ivre* the theme of liberation predominates. Liberation, as we have seen, is the necessary prelude to any kind of religious life, even if it is only liberation from conventional codes of behaviour and conditioned responses. For Rimbaud, the mystic, liberation meant far more than this : it meant complete independence of the world of men. The boat loses its crew and for ten nights rides the seas at its own will. It has no nostalgia for the homely lights of the mainland and feels with pleasure that the green waters wash from it "des taches de vins bleus et des vomissures"*—symbols representing the mainland from which the boat has come, the region of common experience which the poet has transcended.

When the rudder of the boat is washed away its drunken voyage really begins. It undergoes a series of increasingly fantastic and horrifying experiences or visions, and believes that it has been initiated into the esoteric mysteries. In the line

" . . . j'ai vu quelquefois ce que l'homme a cru voir"†

the analogy with Rimbaud himself is transparently clear. The sequence of sensational experiences gives way to a mood of doubt when the boat becomes conscious of itself and begins to wonder about the validity of these hallucinatory experiences, these visions which are of the mind alone and unrelated to actuality. It longs for Europe, for the familiar, and realises that throughout its adventures its

* "the stains of blue wines and vomitings."

† "sometimes I've seen what men believe they can recall."

real Vigour has been dormant. The concluding three stanzas of the poem express the stages which Rimbaud passed through after his disillusionment: utter despair followed by a renewed faith in the familiar, the particular and concrete, and finally his abdication of his position as a *voyant* which led ultimately to his quitting poetry in favour of the coffee trade:

"Mais vrai, j'ai trop pleuré ! Les Aubes sont navrantes.
Toute lune est atroce et tout soleil amer :
L'âcre amour m'a gonflé de torpeurs enivrantes.
O que ma quille éclate ! O que j'aille à la mer !

Si je désire une eau d'Europe, c'est la flâche
Noire et froide où vers le crépuscule embaumé
Un enfant accroupi plein de tristesses, lâche
Un bateau frêle comme un papillon de mai.

Je ne puis plus, baigné de vos langueurs, ô lames,
Enlever leur sillage aux porteurs de cotons,
No traverser l'orgueil des drapeaux et des flammes,
Ni nager sous les yeux horribles des pontons."

"And yet, I've wept too much. The dawns are sharp distress,
All moons are baleful and all sunlight harsh to me
Swollen by acrid love, sagging with drunkenness—
Oh, that my keel might rend and give me to the sea !

If there's a water in all Europe that I crave,
It is the cold, black pond where 'neath the scented sky
Of eve a crouching infant, sorrowfully grave,
Launches a boat as frail as a May butterfly.

Alas, I can no more—steeped, waves, in your long trance—
Steal the wind from the lofty cotton-clippers' sails,
Nor venture 'midst the flags' and pennants' arrogance,
Nor swim beneath the frightful eyes of floating gaols !"[7]

Rimbaud probably underwent two major experiences of disillusionment. After the first, the one we have traced, he

human experiences and therefore fallible and unfitted for revealing truth and stripping away illusion. His departure was going to be a complete change, the noises and visions of the human world were to be supplanted by new sound and the "affection" of pure being.

But *Départ* expresses only the impulse towards the mystical life, and we have to look elsewhere, namely at the *Illuminations* called *Solde* and *Veillées*, to discover what this life meant to the poet. *Solde* (*Sale*) represents symbolically the psychological fact of the mystic's absolute gamble, his staking his shirt on eternity. Only by renouncing everything by an act of will can he come to possess everything by an act of grace. The sale is exhaustive, it is the whole of the poet's world that is being sold, and for Rimbaud that meant the whole universe. For him the sale was "l'occasion, unique, de dégager nos sens,"* and its purpose was to create in himself the capacity for making an "Élan insensé et infini aux splendeurs invisibles, aux délices insensibles."† He had come to realise by now what all mystics, east and west, realise, namely that the transcendent life cannot be arrested by the human will, but rather germinates when that will has been suspended, when a man has made himself as an empty vessel which patiently waits to be filled. *Solde* illustrates the truth of one of the paradoxical statements that T. S. Eliot makes in *East Coker*:

> "In order to possess what you do not possess
> You must go by the way of dispossession."

Veillées (*Vigils*) is concerned with the stage in the mystical process which follows that of renunciation, the stage of patient watching and waiting. The vigil must be a period of intense concentration, but without strain or passion, by a man at once detached and in the full possession of his faculties. If this condition is fulfilled the watcher may be

* "the unique opportunity of freeing our senses."
† "Wild and infinite leap to invisible splendour, to immaterial delights."

rewarded with a sudden and unpredictable vision. The concluding words of the poem, "seule vue d'aurore, cette fois",*
constitute a symbol for any of the visions which make up the
Illuminations, each of which came unpredictably to the poet
in his solitude.

I have previously spoken of the mystic as a man primarily
concerned not with visions, but with experiencing union
with God. Throughout his life Arthur Rimbaud had a profound need for God, though at a very early stage he revolted
against conventional religiosity, and declared in his poem
Le Mal (*Evil*) that :

"Il est un Dieu, qui rit aux nappes damassées
  Des autels, à l'encens, aux grands calices d'or ;
  Qui dans le bercement des hosannah s'endort,

Et se réveille, quand des mères, ramassées
  Dans l'angoisse, et pleurant sous leur vieux bonnet noir,
  Lui donnent un gros sou lié dans leur mouchoir !"

"He is a God who sees it all, and laughs aloud
  At damask altar-cloths, incense and chalices,
  Who falls asleep lulled by adoring liturgies,

And wakens when some mother, in her anguish bowed,
  And weeping till her old black bonnet shakes with grief,
  Offers him a big sou wrapped in her handkerchief."[8]

A God who responded to passion rather than to conventional worship was acceptable to the young poet, but as he
grew older he grew steadily away from the Christian religion.
His attitude to Christ was unequivocally expressed in the
last stanza of *Les Premières Communions* (*The First Communions*), written in July 1871 :

"Christ ! ô Christ, éternel voleur des énergies,
  Dieu qui pour deux mille ans vouas à ta pâleur,
  Cloués au sol, de honte et de céphalalgies,
  Ou renversés, les fronts des femmes de douleur."

* "this time, a solitary vision of dawn."

"O Christ, Christ ! Eternal thief of abundance !
It is two thousand years since your bloodlessness bound
  to its will,
Pinned to the earth, outraged, in an aching of fore-
  heads,
Prostrate beneath you, the brows of our Ladies of
  Sorrow !"[9]

There followed upon this the promethean stage of Rimbaud's spiritual development. No existing concepts of deity
could satisfy him, and, aware of the superhuman creative
powers he possessed, he imagined himself as the equal of
God. In *Nuit de l'Enfer* he went so far as to invite others to
recognise him as such :

"Fiez-vous donc à moi, la foi soulage, guide, guérit.
Tous, venez,—même les petits enfants,—que je vous
console, qu'on répande pour vous son coeur,—le coeur
merveilleux !—Pauvres hommes, travailleurs ! Je ne
demande pas de prières ; avec votre confiance seulement,
je serai heureux."

"Have faith, then, in me, for faith is easement, guidance
and healing. Come all ye—even the little children—that
I may comfort you, that unto all of you His Heart, that
wondrous Heart, may be laid bare. Poor men and
labourers, I ask for no prayers. I shall be happy in your
trust alone."

Rimbaud's most characteristic, and most of his best, work
was done during his promethean period. But, as we have
seen, it was a phase which passed. "J'attends Dieu avec
gourmandise"*, he says in *Mauvais Sang*, and "Je suis telle-
ment délaissé que j'offre à n'importe quelle divine image des
élans vers la perfection."† The divine image which he

* "I await God with greed."
† "I am so forlorn that I make to the first divine image that comes an
offering of urges towards salvation."

finally found himself capable of accepting was certainly far removed from the Christian idea of God. It is apostrophized in the *Illumination* called *A Une Raison* and more fully described in *Génie*. Its chief attributes are power and love—terms which require further elucidation if they are to be understood in the present context. The supreme power to Rimbaud's mind was the power to create, and particularly to create the unprecedented. *A Une Raison* opens with three short paragraphs on this theme:

"Un coup de ton doigt sur le tambour décharge tous les sons et commence la nouvelle harmonie.

"Un pas de toi c'est la levée des nouveaux hommes et leur en marche.

"Ta tête se détourne: le nouvel amour! Ta tête se retourne:—le nouvel amour!"

"A tap with your finger on the drum releases all sounds and begins the new harmony.

"One step of yours, and the new men rise up and march.

"Your head turns aside: new love! Your head turns back: new love!"

The theme of transformation, or of re-creation, is a major one in the *Illuminations*. We have already come across Rimbaud's belief that love must be reinvented, and in the figure of the Genie it is. Rimbaud's concept of deity was always a projection and magnification of the powers in himself which he felt to be divine. In *Matinée d'Ivresse* he had spoken of his very pure love ("très pur amour"), and in *Génie* the fact emerges that love was to his mind the power which enabled the artist to transcend himself, which transformed the world before his eyes, and which enabled him to affirm even what appeared to be terrible. The strong prose rhythms of *Génie* communicate the ecstatic religious experience which the poet had in contemplating this superhuman being, of whom he wrote:

"Il est l'amour, mesure parfaite et réinventée, raison merveilleuse et imprévue, et l'éternité."

"He is love, perfect and reinvented measure, miraculous, unforeseen reason, and eternity."

Though Rimbaud allowed his sister to convert him to the Catholic faith on his death-bed, *Génie* is the fullest expression of his concept of deity during the period of his life with which we are here concerned. The poem does not lend itself to quotation, because its several parts have reference to each other, but one thing is clear from it, namely that to the end of his literary career Rimbaud persisted in identifying the divine and poetic creative processes and in envisaging God in the poet's image.

In conclusion I propose to consider successively the demonic and angelic aspects of Rimbaud's character. Dissatisfied as he was with the conditions of human life with its conventional codes of morality and manners, its lack of vigour and intensity, Rimbaud revolted against it and found that in the type of life which most people would consider sinful and irresponsible he most fully realised himself. He needed above all things to be free, even if he had to suffer for it. His deepest nature urged him to pursue a solitary life, in which his only responsibility was to himself. He considered himself exempt from all moralities, declaring that "La morale est la faiblesse de la cervelle."* He arrogated to himself the right to decide what was and was not lawful, and arrived at the conclusion that anything was permissible that enabled him to attain to the region of the superhuman. He was severe with himself and with others, particularly with Verlaine, whom he regarded as being all too human. Verlaine was by nature weak and vicious, but Rimbaud carried him far deeper into the life of vice than he would ever have gone as a result of his weakness. Rimbaud's compulsion was metaphysical—a thing which Verlaine

---

* "Morality is the weakness of the brain" (*Une Saison en Enfer*).

never understood. He wondered at Rimbaud "faisant de
l'infamie une gloire, de la cruaté un charme",* and was
at once outraged and fascinated by his violence. Together
they indulged in orgies of dissipation, and they quarrelled
and fought bitterly. Verlaine's verdict on his young friend
as expressed by Rimbaud himself in that remarkably
objective *Délires I* was that he was an unaccountable,
inhuman being : "C'est un Démon vous savez, *ce n'est pas un
homme.*"†

In the opening paragraphs of *Une Saison en Enfer*
Rimbaud gives his own account of the origin of his
demonism, which, as I have said, was simply a desire to
transcend the human.

"Je parvins à faire s'évanouir dans mon esprit toute
l'espérence humaine. Sur toute joie pour l'étrangler j'ai
fait le bond sourd de la bête féroce.

"J'ai appelé les bourreaux pour, en périssant, mordre
la crosse de leurs fusils. J'ai appelé les fléaux, pour
m'étouffer avec le sable, le sang. Le malheur a été mon
dieu. Je me suis allongé dans la boue. Je me suis
séché à l'air du crime. Et j'ai joué de bons tours à la
folie."

"I succeeded in extinguishing within myself every
human hope. With the stealthy pounce of a wild beast
I rushed upon every joy, to strangle it.

"I summoned the executioners, that, dying, I might
bite their rifle-butts. I summoned all plagues, to choke me
in sand and blood. Adversity was my God. I sprawled in
the mud, and dried myself in the air of crime. I played
some fine tricks upon madness."

For Sartre "Hell is other people", but Rimbaud could
experience hell only in solitude, when all connections with
other people had been severed and he became himself a

---

* "boasting of infamy, making a magic spell of cruelty."
† "He is a demon, you know, *he is not a man.*"

world. Such was the purpose of the de-humanising process explained in the above quotation. But why did he wish to experience hell? Because he wished to explore himself thoroughly and knew that certain regions of the human soul are accessible only by way of extreme and violent experience. He felt hell within himself as a potential reality which he wanted to make actual. For Rimbaud the psychological reality behind the idea of suffering in hell was self-confrontation. At the end of *Nuit de l'Enfer* occurs the sentence "Je suis caché et je ne le suis pas."* This paradox may be interpreted as meaning simply that in hell he is hidden from the world but not from himself. When a man is persecuted in the world, judged according to some rigid code of behaviour, he can retain a sense of the absolute value of his own life and principles in contradiction to the values of the world. But when he confronts his own conscience and finds himself lacking, when he analyses himself with fearful objectivity and apprehends the primitive chaos that underlies his conscious life and into which he may at any time relapse, there remains no way of escape from despair. This is exactly what Rimbaud did. Throughout *Une Saison en Enfer* we find him dwelling upon his primitive, bestial nature. "Je suis de race inférieure de toute éternité"† he says, and "je n'ai jamais été chrétien ; je suis de la race qui chantait dans le supplice ; je ne comprends pas les lois ; je n'ai pas le sens moral, je suis une brute."‡

The state of mind in which *Une Saison en Enfer* had its origin corresponds to the mystic's "Dark Night of the Soul", the stage in his development when he feels himself to be abandoned by God and forever bound to the world. The whole work is a cry from the depths of the human soul and it testifies to man's need of God when external

---

* "I am hidden, and I am not hidden."

† "I have been of an inferior race since all eternity."

‡ "I was never a Christian. I belong to the race that used to sing under torture. I do not understand laws. I have no moral sense, I am an animal."

F

circumstances or a willed inner crisis place him in an extreme situation.

The primitive consciousness which Rimbaud uncommonly possessed, and because of which he regarded himself as a brute in *Une Saison en Enfer* and in his poetic theory sought to return to the emotional source of language, was also in part responsible for the angelic aspect of his character. He was a being free from original sin. "Apprécions sans vertige l'étendue de mon innocence",* he writes in *Mauvais Sang*, fully conscious of his exception. He was exempt from the common lot of mankind, because in a way he did not belong to the modern world, but had his roots deeply bedded in the dark, pre-Christian past. The distinction between good and evil, so much emphasised by Christianity, was meaningless to him. That is why he regarded himself as not being responsible before any moral concept. In *Matinée d'Ivresse* he wrote:

"On nous a promis d'enterrer dans l'ombre l'arbre du bien et du mal, de déporter les honnêtetés tyranniques, afin que nous amenions notre très pur amour."

"They promised me they would bury in the darkness the tree of good and evil, and deport tyrannical codes of honesty so that I may bring forward my very pure love."

Though the world did not allow Arthur Rimbaud to live, on the social level at any rate, in accordance with his nature, it made no incursions upon his solitude. It is because he did not belong to the world and was untainted by it, because he was beyond good and evil, or rather before them, and because he had divine creative power allied to the "very pure love" of which he speaks, that Rimbaud occupies a singular position among modern poets (all poets, in fact, since the Renaissance), a position which the concept of the Angel perhaps best encompasses.

* "Let us contemplate without dizziness the huge extent of my innocence."

The first impression which the arrogant, God-defying and ridiculously youthful poet gives is one of complete self-absorption and unconcern whether the rest of the world survives or perishes. This impression is contradicted by several passages, notably in *Délires I*, where he says to Verlaine in a solemn and prophetic manner : "il faudra que je m'en aille, très loin, un jour. Puis il faut que j'en aide d'autres : c'est mon devoir."* Behind the mask of violence there was in Rimbaud something of the tenderness and gentleness of the saint. Detachedly and compassionately he looked down upon those who suffered from the trials and torments of human existence, and with his "very pure love" tried to comfort and console them. The Verlaine-figure tells how Rimbaud behaved when the angelic aspect of his nature took precedence :

"Parfois il parle, en une façon de patois attendri, de la mort fait repentir, des malheureux qui existent certaine-ment, des travaux pénibles, des départs qui déchirent les coeurs. Dans les bouges où nous nous enivrions, il pleurait en considérant ceux qui nous entouraient, bétail de la misère. Il relevait les ivrognes dans les rues noires. Il avait la pitié d'une mère méchante pour les petits enfants.—Il s'en allait avec des gentillesses de petite fille au catéchisme."

"Sometimes he speaks, in a sort of tender jargon, of death that brings repentance, of all the miserable people there must be in the world, of painful labours and heart-rending partings. In the hovels where we used to get drunk he would weep as he watched those around us, poverty's cattle. He would lift up drunkards from the black streets. He had a wicked mother's pity on little children. He would go about with the pretty airs of a little girl at Sunday school."

* "I shall have to go away, far away, one day. Then I must go to the help of others: It is my duty."

The figure that emerges from this chapter is a complex of contradictory characteristics. The partisan critic may resolve these as he chooses; their true resolution, if there is one, is lost in those seventeen years of complete silence which followed Rimbaud's abandonment of literature. I have been concerned here only with presenting the man in all his diversity, and for that reason have had to quote liberally from his writings. The point I wish to make is that, like Yeats, he was a divided man, but much more of an extremist, and that in pursuing his contradictory inclinations to their extremes he passed momentarily beyond division and experienced the vision of the mystic and the compassionate detachment of the saint.

One final paradox: though by reason of his exception from original sin and his affinity with primitive races Rimbaud did not belong to the modern world, he was in another sense very much a child of his age, and his life epitomises and brings home to us the dilemma of modern man. Because he was uncompromising, he was silenced. Because he could find no tradition in which to root himself his literary career was short. The inadequacy of Christianity was, he said, the "source de mes divagations spirituelles".* He turned to the East and its first eternal wisdom, and found it "un rêve de paresse grossière!"† His spiritual home was among primitive, amoral races, but he was a conscious being living in the modern world and unwilling to renounce the responsibility which that position entailed. "Il faut etre absolument moderne",‡ he declared; and it was because being absolutely modern and being bigger than mankind were incompatibles, that Rimbaud forsook literature in his twentieth year and devoted the rest of his life to arduous and dangerous trading in an arid and non-Christian part of the world. Among his literary remains

* "source of my spiritual vagrancies" (*Une Saison en Enfer*).

† "a dream of gross indolence" (*Une Saison en Enfer*).

‡ "One must be absolutely up to date" (*Une Saison en Enfer*).

was this implied indictment of the liberal, democratic
and humanistic civilization which had forced him to this
extremity :

"La science, la nouvelle noblesse! Le progrès. Le
monde marche! Pourquoi ne tournerait-il pas?"

"Science, the new nobility; and progress. . . . The
world is on the march—why shouldn't it march in
circles?"

CHAPTER FIVE

RILKE: THE VISIONARY INDIVIDUALIST

"He who no longer finds what is great in God, will find
it nowhere—he must either deny or create it."[1]

NIETZSCHE.

I

UP TO THE PRESENT point we have seen man, as represented by the four poets dealt with, maintaining unified consciousness so long as he remained in harmony with nature, but with his awakening to the metaphysical becoming divided within. In Rimbaud that division was carried to an extreme, and we saw how, for moments at any rate, that poet passed beyond division and attained to a clear and unified vision of the world. The subjects of these final chapters are two poets who have endeavoured to build up for themselves an integral and consistent *Weltanschauung*, to bring their poetic function to terms with their life in the modern world. Both Rilke and Mr. Eliot had their moments of illumination, but the doctrinal foundations of these moments were securely laid, and the poetry produced strengthened and was strengthened by the philosophical premises in which it was rooted.

These premises were very different in each of these two poets. It is true, I think, to say that Rilke's is a poetical philosophy, whereas Mr. Eliot writes philosophical poetry. The distinction means that the ideas of Rilke have validity only in their poetical context or as the expression of a psychological condition, whereas Mr. Eliot's ideas are more applicable and acceptable as an interpretation of life. But the philosophies of both poets have been subjected to, and in part formed by, the same conditions. Both were men of developed consciousness confronting the problem of the poet's existence in the modern world and discovering, each for himself, a philosophical position which affirmed that existence and upheld the spiritual values which they mutually believed to be meaningful. For all their differences Rilke and Mr. Eliot have one thing in common : they are two modern poets, perhaps the only two, who have succeeded to a considerable extent in emerging from the chaos, both internal and external, which is the inheritance of man in our time.

Of modern poets Rilke is the great solitary, the preeminent individualist. All his major ideas have the common object of leading a man back into himself. The idea of transformation of the external into an inner reality, of a man dying his 'personal death' and thereby achieving self expression in the last act of his life, of unrequited love being nobler than love which finds its natural satisfaction : all these major Rilkean ideas contribute to the establishment of an ideal for man which consists in his remaining always concentrated within himself and rejecting any kind of experience which would diminish the intensity of his effort to apprehend the infinite. It can be shown, therefore, that Rilke's ideas, like those of most men, were conditioned by, or even were an expression of, his psychological constitution. He was a natural solitary. He didn't need other people ; in fact he needed to keep them at a distance, hence the voluminousness of his correspondence. Throughout his life numerous women loved him, but he was incapable of really loving any of them in return. A recurrent theme in his intimate writings is his own inadequacy in love, and in his poetry he is extravagant in his admiration of the selflessness of woman's devotion. Rilke's world was bounded on the one hand by the material form of the art-object (das Ding), and on the other by the immaterial realm of Platonic Ideas (such as the sublime concept of the Angel in the *Duino Elegies*). Between these two extremes there was little room for the human, and indeed in few of Rilke's poems are the emotions expressed ordinary human ones. It is chiefly by reason of the distinctive nature of his emotional experiences that Rilke impresses us as being a religious poet. His type of sensibility is, we feel, an advance in consciousness; and the reading of his works opens up for us a beyond, a more than human ideal in relation to which the self-gratifying activities of our normal lives pale into insignificance.

Sublime is an appropriate epithet for the Rilkean concepts. None of his ideas will bear critical examination from the philosophical standpoint, but we have seen how they are all deducible from his psychological condition as a solitary; and for each of us in those significant moments of our lives when we are thrown back upon ourselves the value of these concepts in giving life meaning is immeasurable. Rilke was one of the very few great myth-makers of modern times. If he started as a symbolist he succeeded more than did any other poet of that school in creating universally valid images for those processes of the human spirit which urge man to be continually aspiring beyond himself.

It took many years for Rilke's powers to develop fully. He was not a dogmatic poet, and he never assumed the promethean mask that Yeats and Rimbaud so proudly wore. The power of his mature verse is the power born out of weakness being painfully overcome. He is distinguished from the poets previously dealt with by the degree of his receptivity. He always regarded himself as a servant rather than a master; as the servant of powers before which man must humble himself, and which confer upon him the greatest imaginable honour if they use him as a vehicle through which to express themselves. The mature Rilke resembles in some respects the young Rimbaud. Both established outposts in the unconscious from which they cast light upon previously unexpressed intuitions and emotional states. Both believed in the power of the Word to transmute the evanescent world into durable form. Both were mystics, though of a different order: for Rilke expression was all, whereas for Rimbaud experience was all. Rimbaud's insight may have been profounder and his experience more intense, but it was Rilke who took over where he left off the task of translating that experience and insight into images assimilable by the human intelligence. The gradualness of Rilke's development as compared with that of Rimbaud is no indication of his inferiority. Indeed it may be regarded as a reason for the fact that his poetry fills our stomach, so to speak, more than the rather elusive writings of the boy-poet. What the latter was born to, Rilke had to win by a lifetime's labour and therefore valued more.

II

As a rule the solitary retreats from the world into himself by an act of choice. Less frequently he is a congenital solitary; that is to say, his interests and responses are abnormal. He is born, as it were, without the antennae which normally relate the individual to his fellow men and to the world around him. He is in a vacuum, bounded by the walls of his selfhood. The experience of this situation is common in adolescence, but it is usually quickly outgrown as the horizon of the external world expands and reveals hitherto unsuspected correspondences with the newly discovered subjective feelings. It is rare indeed for a person to be constitutionally solitary to as late a stage in his life as Rilke was. Psychologists may explain the fact by referring to the conditions of his home background in childhood and to the deep impression made upon him by the bitter years spent at the military academy at St. Pölten. No doubt there is some truth in this explanation, but it ignores the fact that Rilke's solitariness was a necessary condition of his being the type of artist he was. Thomas Mann's Tonio Kröger comes to mind as a comparison; Tonio Kröger who felt the "gnawing, surreptitious hankering for the bliss of the commonplace,"[2] who was divided into two selves, the one longing to take the lovely Ingeborg Holm to wife and settle with her in a life in the conventional pattern, and the other realising that his destiny lay in the tracing of quite a different pattern, and that he was committed by it to the solitary life. Rilke and Tonio Kröger were both congenital solitaries, cut off from the world of men because their ideal was pitched beyond it and all their interests and responses were conditioned by

their relation to that ideal. As Rilke wrote in a letter to
Princess Marie von Thurn und Taxis-Hohenlohe in 1912:
"my fate is, as it were, to pass by the human, to reach the
uttermost, the edge of the earth."[3]

The congenital solitary has to establish some sort of relationship with the world, for he cannot be creative in a
vacuum. This can be a painfully slow process. It was so with
Rilke. Wholly bound up within himself, he had no experience out of which to write. Like Niels Lyhne in the novel of
that name by Jacobsen which he so admired, he wrote his
early poetry "out of an aesthetic personality that found
spring abundant, the sea vast, love erotic and death melan-
choly. He himself had got no further by means of this
poetry, he only made the poems."[4] It was Jacobsen, however, who first led Rilke out of himself. He, Rodin and
Nietzsche were the three great formative influences in the
poet's life. Jacobsen's main contribution was to confirm
Rilke's intuition that the world of nature was in some way
co-extensive with the world within him, and that in nature
he might find symbols to express those stirrings in his soul
which had hitherto been elusive and inexpressible.

In 1899 Rilke first visited Russia, the country which he
came to regard as his spiritual home. The passionate and
mystical temperament of its people, the vastness and sombre
beauty of its landscapes, evoked responses within him which
he had not before experienced, and he wrote in a letter that:
"I feel during these days that *Russian* things will give me
the names for those most terrible pieties of my being, which,
ever since childhood, have been longing to enter my art."
The influence upon him of his first experience of Russia is
evident in his first important poetical work, *Das Stundenbuch*. Here Rilke reveals himself as a God-intoxicated man.
The poems celebrate the greatness of God ("Gott, du bist
gross"),* His omnipresence and identity with all life, and
seek to express the poet's mystical states in which he felt
himself to be intimate with the deity.

Rilke's God-relationship at this stage was such as we have

* "God, you are vast."

not come across before in this book. It was a relationship of
mutual dependence and of a passionate love on the part of
the poet. There is no arrogance or presumption, no solicita-
tion or expectation of any benefit except that of remaining
in solitary communion with God. The poems speak with a
passion which can only be compared with that of the
Spanish mystics St. Teresa and St. John of the Cross. The
strong, brooding rhythms of the lines communicate an
almost sensuous experience. God is conceived as needing
the poet just as much as He is needed by him.

> "Was wirst du tun, Gott, wenn ich sterbe?"

> "What will you do, God, when I die?"[5]

he asks, and elsewhere he addresses the deity as "Du,
Nachbar Gott",* attributes human needs to him, and
emphasises the fact that their relationship is one of mutual
dependence:

> "Und wenn du etwas brauchst, ist keiner da,
>   um deinem Tasten einen Trank zu reichen:
>   ich horche immer. Gid ein kleines Zeichen.
>   Ich bin ganz nah."[3]

> "And should you need a drink, no one is there
>   to reach it to you, groping in the dark.
>   Always I harken. Give but a small sign.
>   I am quite near."

The mystic, with his powerful subjective experience of
God, has always been inclined to conflict with the Church
and its dogmas. Very often, however, the Church manages,
after his death, to assimilate the mystic within its tradition,
and he becomes duly canonized. But Rilke, though obviously influenced in some ways by the Catholic tradition,
moved further and further away from it as he grew older.

* "You, neighbour God."

Even in the early sequence of poems *The Life of the Virgin Mary*, Mary is not divine as the Virgin Mother of the Catholic Faith is divine. For Rilke she served as a symbol of purity, and was nothing more. Rilke found all the dogmas of Christianity quite inacceptable. In the *Stundenbuch* he envisages a time in the future when there will be

" . . . keine Kirchen, welche Gott umklammern
wie einen Flüchtling und ihn dann bejammern
wie ein gefangenes und wundes Tier."

"No churches to encircle God as though
he were a fugitive, and then bewail him
as if he were a captured wounded creature."

The Church was an obstacle, and indeed so was Christ, to man's direct experience of God. For Christ the man, the sufferer, he had great sympathy and respect, but he had no time or patience for Christ as the Church represented him, the mediator between God and Man. The mediator could only be useful for those who felt an abyss between themselves and God. As we have seen, this was no part of Rilke's experience. He did not need to approach God by any roundabout way, for, as he said in a letter to Ilse Jahr, "why should those go a-travelling who have never left him?"

Rilke was constitutionally averse to the essence of Christianity, for he saw it as a world- and life-negating religion which pirated to a Beyond the benefits which man should enjoy in the present. No less than Whitman, Rilke conceived it as his task to "exalt the present and the real," and a religion which required man to stake his hopes on a future life and abjure the things of the earth and the experiences of the senses was anathema to him. In the *Stundenbuch* he had addressed God as "du Ding der Dinge",* and through all the gradations of his philosophical and religious position he retained his original attachment to the tangible world, the world of *things*.

* "You thing of things."

Rilke maintained this attitude towards Christianity throughout his life. This meant that he had to elaborate a personal mythology in order to express his religious experience in its mature stages. The gentle, intimate God of the *Studenbuch*, and of such poems as *Herbst* in *Das Buch der Bilder*, could not satisfy the poet for long. He was inevitably superseded by the Angel of the *Duino Elegies*. The Angel is *schrecklich* (*terrible*), but is nevertheless a concept which, because it represents an ideal, is capable of supplying an ethic for life, whereas the comfortable, 'neighbour' god of the early poems could only provide an opiate. What relates the different ideas of deity which Rilke entertained at different stages in his life is that they were all ideals to be praised, celebrated and loved, inner values of the spirit which, because they were personal, needed no external verification. St. Anselm's 'ontological proof' of the existence of God, and also the arguments which Descartes adduces in his *Meditations*, would both have been meaningless to a poet for whom God was "a direction of the heart."

The themes of departure, progress and change are recurrent in Rilke's poetry. The poem on *The Departure of the Prodigal Son* in *Neue Gedichte* contemplates the unpredictability of the future prospect the possibility of dying alone and destitute in a foreign land, but ends with the question

"Ist das der Eingang eines neuen Lebens?"

"Is this the entrance into some new life?"

The implied answer is, of course, yes. The departure of the prodigal son is symbolical, as is the departure of Joseph Knecht in Hermann Hesse's novel *Das Glasperlenspiel*, of the entrance onto a higher level existence such as that intimated by Rimbaud in his *Illumination*, *Départ*. Towards the end of his life Rilke wrote one of his *Sonette an Orpheus* on the same theme. The poem opens with the imperative: "Wolle die Wandlung",* and contains the line

* "Choose to be changed."

"Was sich ins Bleiben verschliesst, schon ists das Erstarrte,"

"That which would stay what it is renounces existence."

As with Yeats, it was his will to be changed, to progress, step by step, towards complete self-realisation, that made Rilke, after a not very promising start in the Romantic vein, a major religious poet. His life was purposeful, for he had unexplored realms of spiritual experience to conquer and express, and a fitting epitaph to it would be the last line of his eighth *Duino Elegy*:

"So leben wir und nehmen immer Abschied"

"We live our lives, for ever taking leave."

Paris and Rodin exercised a profound influence on the young Rilke and contributed much to his spiritual development. He first went to Paris in 1902, when he had already composed the first two parts of *Das Stundenbuch* and his *Fruhe Gedichte*, to write a monograph on Rodin's work. He often visited the great sculptor at his home at Meudon, and after some time became a sort of private secretary to him, relieving him of the burden of his correspondence. It was from Rodin that Rilke learnt the importance of *things*, of the art-object as the prototype of all permanence and perfection. He also learnt the great lesson that poetry, no less than sculpture, should be a craft, and the poet a workman. Hitherto he had relied on inspiration, but Rodin's example gave him quite a different attitude to his art. Soon after his arrival in Paris he communicated his discoveries in a letter to his wife Clara:

"You should not think of wanting to do anything, you should only try to build up your own means of expression so as to say everything. . . . This is the essential, that you should not stop at dreams, at intentions, at being in the mood, but that you should transpose everything into *things* with all your strength."

The result was that Rilke's next book of poems, *Neue Gedichte*, though it lacked the unity of subject of *Das Stundenbuch*, was nevertheless a great advance in technique. In the work of Cézanne, as well as that of Rodin, he had found a parallel for what he wanted to achieve in poetry, namely *objectivity*. The artist, he said, should not paint: I love this; but rather: here it is. He should not *judge*, but should be content to *say*. Rilke felt, rightly, that his early poetry had been vitiated by being excessively subjective, and that, fine though many of his effects may have been, he had not succeeded in finding a symbolism which would express his inner experiences naturally, without giving the effect of his having assumed a poetic pose. He realised now that poetry could only be written out of experience which had been completely assimilated. As he wrote in his novel *The Notebook of Malte Laurids Brigge*: "It is the memories themselves that matter. Only when they have turned to blood within us, to glance and gesture, nameless *and no longer to be distinguished from ourselves*—only then can it happen that in a most rare hour the first word of a poem rises in their midst and goes forth from them."[6] [Italics mine.]

There is a passage in the second *Requiem* poem in which Rilke clearly states his new poetical *credo*. The important thing, he says, is not only to express feeling, but to *shape* it. The poet should be like the anonymous workmen who carved the Gothic cathedrals, and, seeking no personal expression, "transposed themselves into the constant stone." What Rilke was aiming at, and what from now on he constantly accomplished, was a complete integration of the poetical image and the subjective experience. In *Neue Gedichte* the Rilkean world becomes clearly defined; the peculiar climate of sensibility in which one finds oneself on reading the *Duino Elegies* and the *Orpheus Sonnets* has been evolved. In this volume Rilke first expressed some of the ideas he was to develop in his maturer work, and, what is equally important, he made great progress in building up his means of expression "so as to say everything."

In the title to the present chapter I have called Rilke a

visionary individualist.* The extent to which he was an
individualist will by now be apparent, but the word
"visionary" has yet to be defined in this context. Rilke's
visions were not dynamic apocalypses of the Blakean type,
but rather subtle, but no less vivid, apprehensions of existence as pure being and of the correspondences subsisting
between his inner states and the external, natural world. His
mysticism consisted in the expression of marginal conditions
of human feeling, intuitions of the essential relatedness of
the human and natural worlds and the cosmos as a whole. It
would be inaccurate, though, to speak of him as a nature
mystic. "I do not think," he wrote in a letter, "anybody has
ever experiencèd more vividly to what an extent art goes
against Nature; it is the most passionate inversion of the
world, the return journey from infinity on which you
encounter all the honest earthly things." Art could not proceed from nature, he said elsewhere, without despair, without a Fall. It is important to establish this point in order to
distinguish Rilke's attitude to nature from that of the first
two poets dealt with in this book. Rilke had no Rousseau-
esque sentiments about nature. He saw in it as clearly as
did Jacob Boehme, the *Ungrund*, the primal, unconscious
chaos (witness the third *Duino Elegy*); but yet, trustingly, he
submitted himself to its direction. His mystical experiences
were not of the kind that are attained by means of asceticism
or rigorous disciplines. They were 'given' to him, and were
independent of his volition. As he wrote to Ellen Key during
his early days in Paris :

> "I must wait for the ringing in the silence, and I know
> that if I force the ringing, then it really won't come.
> Sometimes it is there and I am the master of my depths,
> which open out radiant and beautiful and shimmering in
> the darkness."

Rilke wrote several prose descriptions of his religious
experiences, the most notable of which is a fragment called

* The term was, I believe, first used by Mr. Stephen Spender in his book
The Creative Element.

Erlebnis (*Experience*). This recounts the experience which precipitated the composition of the first *Duino Elegies* in 1912. Walking in the garden of the Schloss Duino with a book, he chanced to recline into the forked branches of a tree,

"and in this position immediately felt himself so agreeably supported and so amply reposed, that he remained as he was, without reading, completely received into nature, in an almost unconscious contemplation. Little by little his attention awoke to a feeling he had never known : it was as though almost imperceptible vibrations were passing into him from the interior of the tree. . . . It seemed to him he had never been filled with more gentle motions, his body was being somehow treated like a soul, and enabled to receive a degree of influence which, given the normal apparentness of one's physical conditions, really could not have been felt at all. . . . Nevertheless, concerned as he always was to account to himself for precisely the most delicate impressions, he insistently asked himself what was happening to him then, and almost at once found an expression that satisfied him, saying to himself, that he had got to the other side of Nature. . . . Looking slowly around him, without otherwise changing his position, he recognized it all, recalled it, smiled at it with a kind of distant affection, let it be, like something much earlier that once, in circumstances long gone by, had had a share in his life. His gaze followed a bird, a shadow engaged him, the very path, the way it went on and got lost, filled him with a pensive insight, which seemed to him all the purer in that he knew he was independent of it."[7]

This hypersensitive condition was the characteristic Rilkean religious experience. He attributed it to the Danish poet-hero of his novel, Malte Laurids Brigge, whom he made write in his *Notebook*: "I possess an inner self of which I was ignorant. Everything now passes in thither. What

happens there I do not know." What happens, Rilke would
have been able to tell him, is that everything is transformed, "changed to a handful of Within." Rilke sent an
extract from a diary to the Countess Stauffenberg in 1919
in which he related an experience he underwent in Capri,
when "the call of a bird was simultaneously outside him and
in the depth of his being," and "the Infinite passed into him
from all sides so trustingly that he fancied he could feel the
stars which had come out meanwhile, gently reposing in his
breast." These experiences pass beyond the frontiers of
human sense-experience. In having them the poet realised a
profound and ineffable harmony in the depths of his being.
In following them up and contemplating them in solitude he
derived from these intimations a searching metaphysical
interpretation of human life. Some people may dismiss the
experiences as commonplace psychical phenomena. But the
poetry which Rilke wrote to express and extend his experience cannot be so disposed of. It is one of the most successful
attempts a modern man has made to orientate himself within
his chaotic world. Having briefly outlined his poetic and
religious development we must now turn our attention to the
aspect of Rilke's genius which made him a *modern* poet, with
particular reference to his two major poetical works, the
Duino Elegies and the *Sonnets to Orpheus*.

III

The quotation from Nietzsche's notebook which I used
as the epigraph to this chapter pinpoints both the dilemma
which Rilke confronted as a modern man and poet, and also
the essence of his greatness. When Nietzsche declared that
God is dead, he meant of course the God of Christianity,
and it was a statement that Rilke would have endorsed. The
alternative that Nietzsche presents in the sentence quoted,
either to deny or to re-create greatness, was one which Rilke
faced and had to choose between. Of course, there was really
no question of choice. Denial would involve an abdication of
his position as a poet. He was born a creator, but was at first
overwhelmed at the immensity of his task, which was no less

than to re-create the world and God. There is no doubt that even at the very beginning of his career he clearly apprehended both his historical position and his destined task. He had read Nietzsche, and that philosopher profoundly and permanently influenced his thought. Before the turn of the century he had composed some poems and prose pieces of Nietzschean posturing, but we have to look to his last works, the *Sonnets to Orpheus* and the *Duino Elegies*, to see just how Nietzsche's ideas and attitude became absorbed into the fundamental premises from which all his poetical activity issued. At a first glance Rilke and Nietzsche seem to be very differently constituted, but on closer consideration we see that they had some important things in common: both were solitaries, both were acutely conscious of the bankruptcy of the Christian religion, both were fervent yea-sayers who had nevertheless confronted ultimate nothingness. Nietzsche evolved the concept of the Superman, and Rilke paralleled it with the Angel. The philosopher and the poet shared the heroic task of re-creating and re-spiritualizing a world that was, in Yeats's words, "breaking into fragments", degenerating by reason of the corruption of its values.

Rilke's feelings that life held infinite potentialities, that there was great, unprecedented and challenging work to be done, that he was in on the beginning of new epoch, were expressed by Malte Laurids Brigge in his *Notebook*. On a grey Parisian afternoon the twenty-eight-year-old Danish poet of Rilke's autobiographical novel questioned himself:

"Is it possible . . . that nothing real or important has yet been seen or known or said? Is it possible that mankind has had thousands of years in which to observe, reflect and record, and has allowed these millennia to slip past, like a recess interval at school in which one eats one's sandwich and an apple?

Yes, it is possible.

Is it possible that despite our discoveries and progress, despite our culture, religion and world-wisdom we still remain on the surface of life? Is it possible that we have even covered this surface, which might still have been something, with an incredibly uninteresting stuff which makes it look like drawing-room furniture during summer holidays?

Yes it is possible."

Malte himself, though he realised the urgency of the task, was impotent to undertake the labour of re-creating the world. That is why the prevailing tone of the novel is one of despair and why Rilke later stated that it ought to be read "*against the current*, as it were." But he also believed that from it some few readers might glean a rare and valuable kind of knowledge, "a great, hopeful knowledge demanding active achievement and one arising in the teeth of insuperable obstacles." Of such a kind was the knowledge he had put into the book, and, although he did not take Malte with him, Rilke emerged from the feeling of impotence and despair and set about the active achievement of re-creation which, as he had learnt from Nietzsche and confirmed with his own vision, was the great spiritual task to be done in his time.

The philosopher Martin Heidegger has said that his work has been an attempt to express in philosophical terms the truths which Rilke expressed symbolically in his poetry. It was Heidegger, remember, who defined the human situation as "being exposed to nothingness."* Rilke confronted that nothingness. He experienced both the metaphysical despair of Pascal and the despair at the spiritual desolation of modern life that drove Nietzsche insane, and he came out of that experience with a characteristic phrase on his lips: "dennoch preisen" (praise nevertheless, praise in spite of). It was a phrase that Neitzsche's Zarathustra would have approved. Praise and celebration in the face of and in full consciousness of the facts that had caused other minds to assume an attitude of negativity, was the declared object of both Rilke and Nietzsche. Zarathustra hymns life and the world ecstatically, declaring "Life is a well-spring of

* See p. 72.

delight",[8] and Rilke, commenting in a letter to his wife on Baudelaire's poem *La Charogne*, writes :

> "The vision of the artist had to steel itself so far as to see in terrible and apparently only repulsive things the Existing, which, in common with all other being, *has value*. As little as any selection is permissible to him, so little is it permitted to the creator to turn away from any form of existence whatever : a single rejection anywhere on his part forces him out of the state of grace, makes him wholly sinful."

It was too easy to despair. What was difficult, and therefore challenging, was to affirm life, to be a yea-sayer. Nietzsche and Rilke, believing respectively that they had extended the frontiers of thought and feeling, took upon themselves the task of affirming *the whole*, of accepting and transfiguring pain, suffering and evil.

Rilke's poetry moves between the poles of praise (*Rühmung*) and lament (*Klage*). The two themes, he emphasised, were complementary :

> "Nur im Raum der Rühmung darf die Klage gehn."

> "Only Praise's realm may Lamentation traverse."

The predominant note in the *Duino Elegies* is one of lament, whereas in the *Sonnets to Orpheus* praise predominates. Suffering and pain were experiences which had to be endured, had to be regarded as merely "*one* of the seasons of our interior year", for only when it grew out of such experiences could praise be valid. This is the meaning of the opening lines of the tenth *Elegy*, in which Rilke wishes upon himself an inner condition such as that in which the *Sonnets to Orpheus* were composed :

> "Dass ich dereinst, an dem Ausgang der grimmigen
>   Einsicht,
> Jubel und Ruhm aufsinge zustimmenden Engeln.
> Dass von den klargeschlagenen Hämmern des Herzens

keiner versage an weichen, zweifelnden oder
reissenden Saiten. Dass mich mein strömendes Antlitz
glänzender mache : dass das unscheinbare Weinen
blühe. O wie werdet ihr dann, Nächte, mir lieb sein,
    gehärmte."

"Some day, emerging at last from this terrifying vision,
may I burst into jubilant praise to assenting Angels !
May not one of the clear-struck keys of the heart
fail to respond through alighting on slack or doubtful
or rending strings ! May a new-found splendour appear
in my streaming face ! May inconspicuous Weeping
flower ! How dear you will be to me then, you Nights of
    Affliction."

Praise and lament are not contradictories, they are opposing poles in a condition of the soul which is itself an integral
whole. The opposition between them must not be resolved,
otherwise the whole will be misapprehended and man will
lose his grasp on reality. A central idea in Rilke's thought is
that by not seeing deeply enough into things man creates his
own evil and suffering. The Angel sees things whole, apprehends the polarities of life, sees, in the words of Herakleitos,
that "Good and ill are one."[9] And the *Duino Elegies*, as
Rilke said, are an attempt to see the world as it would appear
to the Angel, to transcend the partial human vision and see
the Whole. Viewed from this angle, death itself becomes
affirmable, for it is regarded as the "unilluminated" side of
life, the side that is turned away from us, but which is,
nevertheless, contiguous with life, an extension of the finite
into the infinite. Pain and suffering can and must be
affirmed likewise. They are not to be regarded as distinct
and independent events, but as constituent parts of a whole
which is good :

"Welchem der Bilder du auch im Innern geeint bist
    (sei es selbst ein Moment aus dem Leben der Pein),
fühl, dass der ganze, der rühmliche Teppich gameint ist."

"Feel, with what pattern soever you're inwardly blended
  (even a scene from the story of Agony),
  feel that the whole, the praisable, carpet's intended."

All Rilke's best work was done in torrents of creativity
which lasted a few days or weeks and then subsided.
Between these times he suffered long periods of depression,
the longest of which was during and immediately after the
1914-18 war. The war completely disintegrated his
spiritual life and rendered him uncreative for a period of
which he must have thought he would never see the end. He
began the *Duino Elegies* in 1912, but it was not until 1922,
after a solitary winter spent gathering his inner forces in the
Château de Muzot in Switzerland, that he was able to complete them. Add to this the fact that he was weakly constituted and suffered from an incurable disease, and certain
aspects of Rilke's thought are thrown into relief.

The unpredictable and intermittent nature of his inspiration, and the sense of complete possession which he had at
those times, caused him to believe that he was being used
by some unfathomable forces. And in being so used, he
believed, human life attained to its fullest realization. The
suffering, the periods of desolation, did not matter; they
served their purpose. Nor did it matter that life was transient; that very fact contributed to make it glorious and
heroic. The important thing was to *be*, and, with full voice,
to affirm:

"Hier, unter Schwindenden, sei, im Reiche der Neige,
  sei ein klingendes Glas, das sich im Klang schon zerschlug.

Sei—und wisse zugleich des Nicht-Seins Bedingung,
  den unendlichen Grund deiner innigen Schwingung,
  dass du sie völlig vollziehst dieses einzige Mal.

Zu dem gebrauchten sowohl, wie zum dumpfen und
    stummen
  Vorrat der vollen Natur, den unsäglichen Summen,
  zähle dich jubelnd hinzu und vernichte die Zahl."

"Here, in this realm of the dwindlers and dregs, be a ringing
glass, which has, even though shivered to pieces, been rung.

Be—and, perceiving in that which is being's negation
merely the infinite ground of your fervent vibration,
beat, through this never-again, to the fullest amount.

To the stock of used-up, as well as of dumb and decaying
things within copious Nature, those sums beyond saying,
count yourself joyfully in and destroy the account."

This was one way of bringing the infinite into life : by sub-
mitting oneself to be used by great natural forces. The weak
and diseased poet was more conscious than are most men of
the precariousness of human life and of man's impotence
when he stood alone. Yet, since God was dead, he was alone.
But this was unthinkable. All Rilke's experiences and intuitions told him that there was a universal harmony and purpose to which man could relate himself, which already
contained him within itself and required only his conscious
co-operation. But the question was, how to develop this consciousness? how apprehend the purpose? how re-create the
world of man to adapt it to this new ideal? There are a
number of agonized questions behind all Rilke's work,
which reveal the dichotomy he felt between man's transient,
physical being and his aspiring, infinite, spiritual self. They
are : "how is it possible to live when the fundamentals of this
our life are completely incomprehensible?" ; "why/have to
be human, and, shunning Destiny,/long for Destiny?" ;
"when shall we exist?" and "Are we really such tremblingly
breakable/things as Destiny tries to pretend?" It was to
provide his answer to these questions that Rilke composed
both the *Elegies* and the *Sonnets*.

In praise, in prayer, in inwardness, human life finds its
justification. The here and now, the finite and immediate,
contains within itself the eternal and the infinite. Man must
accept the transience of his life, for it is a necessary condition
of the work he has to do, the work of transformation, of

"stamping this provisional, perishing earth into himself so deeply, so painfully and passionately, that its being may rise again, 'invisibly', in him." Finding himself in a world which seemed unreal because man's capacity for passion, for feeling about it, had been diminished, Rilke evolved his original and curious idea about the central importance to life of this work of transformation. Man may be a "tremblingly breakable thing", but he is nevertheless entrusted with the responsible task of raising externality towards the Absolute,* and consequently other things look to him for their salvation.

"Und diese, von Hingang
lebenden Dinge verstehn, dass du sie rühmst; vergänglich,
traun sie ein Rettendes uns, den Vergänglichsten, zu.
Wollen, wir sollen sie ganz im unsichtbarn Herzen ver-
    wandeln
in—o unendlich—in uns!"

"These things that live on departure
understand when you praise them: fleeting, they look for
rescue through something in us, the most fleeting of all.
Want us to change them entirely, within our invisible hearts,
into—oh, endlessly—into ourselves!"

What are these "things" that man is required so to trans-form? Quite ordinary things: houses, bridges, fountains, gates, jugs, fruit trees, windows. And in what does the process of transformation consist? In prayer, love, reverence:

"ein einst gebetetes Ding, ein gedientes, geknietes—,
    hält es sich, so wie es ist, schon in Unsichtbare hin."

"one single thing once prayed or tended or knelt to,
    it's reaching, just as it is, into the unseen world."

Prayer was, to Rilke, as to Gerard Manley Hopkins, any work that was lovingly done. For the latter the labour of

* The phrase is Bosanquet's and is quoted by Mr. Leishman.

Felix Randall the farrier "gave God glory" as much as did attendance at communion. He would have agreed with Rilke when he wrote to his wife "what is there truly done that is not prayer?" The process of transformation is analagous to that of prayer. It requires concentrated and passionate attention to the task, a selfless devotion.

It was with this doctrine in mind that, at the beginning of this chapter, I distinguished between Mr. Eliot's philosophical poetry and Rilke's poetical philosophy. It is obvious how the idea of the external world being transformed and given an invisible existence *within* germinated in the mind of the solitary and aesthetic young poet. It was adumbrated as early as 1898, when, in a diary entry, he spoke in the following terms of the solitary of the future :

> "There will be nothing outside him, trees and mountains, clouds and waves will have been but the symbols of those realities which are found in him. Everything has flown together in him."

And in 1903 he said in a letter to Lou Andreas-Salomé, "Only *things* speak to me." In the ninth *Elegy* he tells how from watching a rope-maker in Rome and a potter in Egypt he had learnt "how happy a thing can be, how guileless and ours." And we need only remember also his admiration for Rodin's work and for the sculpture of the Gothic cathedrals to realise how closely bound up with his own aesthetic personality was Rilke's idea of transformation. This does not invalidate the idea, however, but rather removes it from the central position which Rilke afforded it in his philosophy, and makes it, for us, just a symbol of the work of re-spiritualising life which we all need to do if we are to survive the technological age. Nicolas Berdyaev, together with other modern philosophers, has reiterated the truth that "the objectification of spirit" is one of the worst portents in our time, and that it is essential that we should learn to "return the objective world to the sphere of inner existence."[10] This is Rilke's lesson, and we cannot afford to ignore it.

Rilke is often regarded as a solitary who deliberately cut himself off from the world he was born into and created a secure and artistic world around himself. This is quite wrong. I have tried to show that his poetry proceeded from a vision of the spiritual desolation of the modern world as profound as Nietzsche's. Before considering his final emergence from chaos I propose briefly to enter into his dark vision, so that his ultimate note of affirmation may sound the louder through echoing in the depths.

Rilke wrote his version of *The Waste Land*. He called it the *Leid-Stadt* (*City of Pain*), and his account of it occurs in the tenth *Duino Elegy*. He had always felt that the life that most people led was a half-life, with its accent on money and pleasure, and its attempt to exclude suffering and death and all that is mysterious and inexplicable. Conventional religion was repugnant to him, and in the *Leid-Stadt* he imagined the church "as clean/and disenchanted and shut as the Post on a Sunday!" In the fair the people are mechanically and joylessly pursuing pleasure, greedily grasping at distractions and consuming a beer called "deathless". Theirs is a blind, animal existence, lacking all the qualities that make human existence noble and meaningful. And the horror of it is that they think they are happy, they cannot imagine a better condition of life, so completely have they lost their grasp on authentic existence. Again, in the fifth *Elegy*, Rilke takes a similar view of the human situation. A troupe of acrobats serve as a symbol. Endlessly, monotonously, meaninglessly, they spring up from and jump down upon a "threadbare carpet . . . forlornly lost in the cosmos." The carpet symbolises the life of modern man, alienated from God, from reality. Life is meaningful in proportion to its difficulty, but the acrobats have now developed such facility in their performance that it requires no effort of them. The vision in both these *Elegies* is of a world rendered inhuman and mechanical by reason of man's act of shutting himself off from the infinite in order to ensure his momentary comfort and security. It was Rilke's desire in his poetry to open up again the way to the infinite, to extend the contingent and material into the realm of the eternal and spiritual, to make men able to apprehend again *das Offene* (*the open*), and the *reines Wohin* (*pure Whither*), and to exhibit his idea of "this now first *whole*, first *hale* world".

The work of transformation, Rilke said, is consummated in the Angel. The Angel takes all the world into himself, and Rilke imagined it to be his poetic task not only to represent the world seen by the Angel, but also the world seen *in* the Angel. He symbolised his vision as being that of a blind Angel who encompassed all space and was gazing into himself. But is such a vision ever attainable by man, who is perpetually divided against himself? No :

"Nur dem Aufsingenden säglich.
Nur dem Göttlichen hörbar"

"Only a singer could say it.
Only a god could hear."

To represent his vision he used the mythical figure who was both singer and god—Orpheus. With Orpheus "Gesang ist Dasein"—song is existence, and not merely about, or an embellishment upon, existence. But man, so long as "his sense is discord", is prevented from realising this ideal. Hence the question, in the same sonnet : "When shall we *exist*?" And the answer is in effect the same as that provided by the *Elegies* : when we bring about in ourselves the undivided consciousness of the child, the animal, the unrequited lover, the saint or the devoted craftsman. Song is existence, and pure song is only possible for Orpheus, the god. The implication is unmistakable : we must make ourselves gods. Nietzsche also had a poet-god, Apollo, and he likewise preached that man must make himself godlike. In *Neue Gedichte* Rilke wrote a poem on an "Archaic Torso of Apollo" which ends with the imperative :

"denn da ist keine Stelle,
die dich nicht sieht. Du musst dein Leben ändern."

"here is no place
that does not see you. You must change your life."

The injunction might have come from the lips of Zarathustra. Nietzsche and Rilke, inheriting the same spiritually
bankrupt world and feeling themselves responsible for
giving it new values and a new lease of spirituality, created
their own gods and high ideals. They were the myth-makers
of a new epoch, and by now the Superman and the Angel
have become integral with the modern consciousness. The
gods they invented had one thing in common : they were
yea-sayers, praisers of life. Zaruthustra's "Life is a well-
spring of delight" was echoed in the middle of the seventh
Elegy in Rilke's "Hiersein ist herrlich"—"Life here's
glorious"—and these were the hardest affirmations for men
who had seen the horror and chaos just beneath the ordered
surface of life to make.

I propose to let Rilke himself have the last word. The
following *Sonnet to Orpheus* contains the essence of his
thought and attitude to life :

"Wandelt sich rasch auch die Welt
    wie Wolkengestalten,
    alles Vollendete fällt
    heim zum Uralten.

Über dem Wandel und Gang,
    weiter und freier,
    währt noch dein Vor-Gesang,
    Gott mit der Leier,

Nicht sind die Leiden erkannt,
    nicht ist die Liebe gelernt,
    und was im Tod uns entfernt,

ist nicht entschleiert.
    Einzig das Lied überm Land
    heiligt und feiert."

Change though the world may as fast
as cloud-collections,
home to the changeless at last
fall all perfections.

Over the thrust and the throng,
freer and higher,
echoes your preluding song,
god with the lyre.

Sorrow we misunderstand,
love we have still to begin,
death and what's hidden therein

await unveiling.
Song alone circles the land,
hallowing and hailing.

CHAPTER SIX

T. S. ELIOT AND THE 'INTELLECTUAL SOUL'

"Religious truth must be developed from knowledge acquired when our ordinary senses and intellectual operaations are at their highest pitch of discipline. To move one step from this position towards the dark recesses of abnormal psychology is to surrender finally any hope of a solid foundation for religious doctrine."[1]

A. N. WHITEHEAD

I

THE FIVE POETS to whom I have devoted the foregoing chapters would all be regarded by T. S. Eliot as "heretics". We have seen how each of them reacted away from Christianity, finding it unsatisfactory as a living faith and consequently infertile as a source of poetic inspiration. Eliot, on the other hand, after violently attacking the Church in his second (1920) volume of poems, became, in middle age, a faithful and powerful member of the Anglo-Catholic persuasion. Those who are inclined to believe that this act constituted an abdication of his position as a truly modern man, and who suspect that he did it for the sake of the comfort and security that are to be found by the individual who joins the Church, will, I hope, suspend judgment on these matters at least until they have read the present chapter. Of tradition, Eliot said in his early essay *Tradition and the Individual Talent* that "if you want it you must obtain it by great labour." The same is true of religious faith, and the fact that so conscious a modern man as Eliot should see fit to obtain it by great labour should dispose us to be sympathetic and respectful in considering the reasons which led him to adopt the Christian Faith. Probably most of us would fall into his category of "heretics". This, however, is not to be taken as an indictment, or even an expression of intolerance, but rather as a simple fact. Heresy—the retreat from Christian orthodoxy—is a nineteenth-century movement which has been accelerated in the last 50 years, and today the practising Christian is a rare bird among the intelligentsia. Eliot deplores this fact, for he regards it as indicative of the complete disintegration of the Western European cultural tradition. If that tradition perishes, he believes, civilization must likewise perish, and man relapse into barbarism. You cannot sever a culture from its roots and expect it to survive. If that is to happen there will devolve upon the few who are conscious of the situation the responsibility of "redeeming the time : so that the Faith may be preserved alive through the dark ages before us ; to renew and rebuild civilization and save the World from suicide."[2]

It will be clear from the above that Eliot has more of what we might call a social conscience than any of the poets previously considered. Yeats's heroic despair, Rimbaud's abdication, and Rilke's satisfaction with the creations of his own imagination, would all have been impossible for a man with Eliot's historical sense and feeling of responsibility for the future of the culture he had inherited. As we shall shortly see, he was as acutely conscious as any of these poets of the chaotic nature of the world he had been born into ; but over a period of time he managed simultaneously to order his inner life and to turn his attention outwards to consider social and cultural questions and the historical process. The solutions which the other poets found to their predicament were all provisional and personal. They never really managed to emerge from their own depths, and consequently, though they were all profoundly religious men in the subjective sense, none of them concerned himself with the questions of religious doctrine or with religion as an instrument of social cohesion. In studying them we have entered into what Whitehead calls, in the passage quoted as the epigraph to this chapter, "the dark recesses of abnormal psychology." In most cases their abnormality was the inevitable one of the extraordinarily sensitive and creative spirit, and one could justly argue that as poets it was no part of their task to concern themselves with institutional religion and its doctrines or with the welfare of society. But the work of Yeats, Rimbaud and Rilke was affected by social conditions of which each poet was conscious and towards which he assumed a definite attitude. No major poet can ever be purely a poet, and in so far as he has an implicit or explicit attitude towards the world he inhabits, that attitude is amenable to criticism and comparison with others. In criticising, however, we need to bear in mind the particular poet's psychological constitution. The type of religious experience to which Rilke was susceptible made it impossible for him to conform to any institutional religion. Eliot, on the other hand, with his puritanical inheritance, his ordered education in philosophy and the humanities, his intellectual honesty, reverence for tradition and sense of responsibility, needed only, so to speak, to think himself out to his natural conclusion in order to arrive at the Catholic Faith.

Elsewhere[3] I have spoken of Eliot as a saintly man rather than a poet. By this I meant that his poetry seems to have served as a means to his end of self realisation, as an instrument through which to conduct his internal debate. The fact that he has not written any poetry since *Four Quartets* was completed in 1943 seems to lend support to the idea that for him poetry was secondary to his purpose of spiritual self-development. Moreover, as we shall see, that development is in its various stages comparable with that of many Christian saints. But though he was in a sense a vocational saint, it is an over-simplification of the matter to emphasise his saintliness at the expense of his importance as a poet. Eliot has always been a thoroughly professional practitioner of the poetic craft, "occupied with the struggle—which alone constitutes life for the poet—to transmute his personal and private agonies into something rich and strange, something universal and impersonal." If we regard him either as primarily a poet or primarily a religious man we are liable to misunderstand him. I have therefore taken from Eliot's own essay on Pascal an expression which I think more aptly

G

describes him than any other I have seen used. In that essay Eliot speaks of Pascal's despair and disillusion as "essential moments in the progress of the intellectual soul." Eliot understood from personal experience the nature of the intellectual soul and the various stages of its development. The meaning he attached to the term is quite clear from his essays.

A possible misunderstanding which must immediately be disposed of is that the intellectual soul is *aridly* intellectual. D. H. Lawrence's criticism of the "cerebral consciousness" of such poets as Eliot, with its implication that they neglected man's emotional life and spoke from the mind only, rather than from the whole man, was, at least in so far as it concerned Eliot, based upon an incapacity to understand his work. Eliot's refined sensibility and his exceptional degree of consciousness caused religious emotions to take precedence over the more common, primitive emotions that Lawrence so well understood, though these latter are by no means absent from his work. He admits no absolute division between the intellectual and emotional operations, but believes rather that "The poet who 'thinks' is merely the poet who can express the emotional equivalent of thought." To express "the emotional equivalent of thought", indeed to approach those frontiers of consciousness where thought and emotion are no longer distinguishable from each other, and which can only be expressed at all in "hints and guesses" by means of poetic imagery, has been the constant aim of Eliot in his poetry, and *Four Quartets* stands an unsurpassed masterpiece in this literary *genre*. This is one characteristic of the intellectual soul as it manifests itself in Eliot: the belief that "every precise emotion tends towards intellectual formulation." Other characteristics are defined in the Pascal essay to which I have already referred. There we read:

"The majority of mankind is lazy-minded, incurious, absorbed in vanities, and tepid in emotion, and is therefore incapable of either much doubt or much faith; and when the ordinary man calls himself a sceptic or an unbeliever, that is ordinarily a simple pose, cloaking a disinclination to think anything out to a conclusion."

It is in its will to think things out to a conclusion, in the honesty and integrity of its thought, that the intellectual soul distinguishes itself. In the same essay there occurs an account of how a person so constituted comes to accept Catholic Christianity. The words are as true of Eliot's own thought process as of Pascal's:

"The Christian thinker—and I mean the man who is trying consciously and conscientiously to explain to himself the sequence which culminates in faith, rather than the public apologist—proceeds by rejection and elimination. He finds the world to be so and so; he finds its character inexplicable by any non-religious theory: among religions he finds Christianity, and Catholic Christianity, to account most satisfactorily for the world and especially for the moral world within; and thus, by what Newman calls 'powerful and concurrent' reasons, he finds himself inexorably committed to the dogma of the Incarnation. To the unbeliever, this method seems disingenuous and perverse: for the unbeliever is, as a rule, not so greatly troubled to explain the world to himself, nor so greatly distressed by its disorder; nor is he generally concerned (in modern terms) to 'preserve values'."

The intellectual soul, then, is found in the man who is endowed with the metaphysical heed of finding an explanation of the world and his own place in it. He cares for, and in a sense lives by, thought; and this distinguishes him from the generality of mankind. He may start from a feeling of distress at the palpable chaos of the world, or from a desire to maintain what he considers a right standard of values in the world, or, as did Eliot himself, from a combination of these two causes; he ends ultimately by assenting to the dogmas of Catholic Christianity, for that is the conclusion at which anyone starting from such a position and having the will to think things out to their end must inevitably arrive. Faith does not come easily to him; it is not a natural disposition of his soul or an inherited and unquestioned belief, but is arrived at, to quote Whitehead again, "when his ordinary senses and intellectual operations are at their highest pitch of discipline." It is for this reason that I believe that the discoveries and doctrines of the intellectual soul have more universal and practical meaning than those evolved by the psychologically abnormal and philosophically heterodox poets whom we have previously studied. That is why I have chosen to make Eliot the subject of the final chapter of this book. The others may help us individually to overcome the chaos within. He alone has a contribution to make, which is of a comprehensive if undeveloped nature, to the responsible task of conscious men in all ages, and in ours particularly; namely, the forming of the future.

II

On the rare occasions when he appears in the popular Press, Eliot emerges as an enigmatic figure; as when, after the first production of *The Confidential Clerk* at Edinburgh in 1953, he exasperated the journalists by telling them that the play meant "whatever you want it to mean." Among the intelligentsia there is much curiosity but little knowledge as regards his personal life. One hears rumours about his daily tube or bus journey from Chelsea to Russell Square, and a story (probably legendary) about the occasion when he and Gilbert Harding happened to be in the same crowded compartment in an underground train, the poet inconspicuous behind his copy of *The Times*, the unfortunate radio personality the centre of discreet attention. He has been attacked and applauded by various critics, constantly misinterpreted and misrepresented, but has joined battle with none and never washed his linen in public. To add to the confusion he has, as Old Possum, given us his *Book of Practical Cats*. In 1927 he remarked humorously that he was already used to "having my personal biography reconstructed from passages which I got out of books, or which I invented out of nothing because they wounded well; and to having my biography ignored in what I *did* write from personal experience." As a further warning to the critic there is the famous statement in *Tradition and the Individual Talent* about the separateness of "the man who suffers and the mind which creates." In spite of all this, however, I propose in the pages that follow to relate the man and his poetry and to trace through the poetry the stages in the spiritual biography of the poet.

Age is a recurrent theme in Eliot's early poetry, indeed up to *Ash Wednesday*, which appeared in 1930. The ineffectual J. Alfred Prufrock sighs

> "I grow old. . . . I grow old . . .
> I shall wear the bottoms of my trousers rolled."

Gerontion is

> "An old man in a draughty house
> Under a windy knob."

Tiresias, the observer in *The Waste Land*, is an

> "Old man with wrinkled female breasts."

And that most personal of Eliot's poems, *Ash Wednesday*, opens with a passage in which he asks:

> "(Why should the agèd eagle stretch its wings?)
> Why should I mourn
> The vanished power of the usual reign?"

Age is a symbol of futility, sterility, time profitlessly spent, civilization meaninglessly lapsing into decay. It is consistent with the mood of disillusion in the early poems. It disappears from the poetry he wrote after his conversion to Catholicism.

In his essay on *Humanism and the Religious Attitude*, T. E. Hulme says: "I should say that the starting point for the religious attitude was always the kind of discussion you find in Pascal (Fragment 139. Brunschvig edition)."⁴ We have already noted certain points of similarity between Eliot and Pascal. In the fragment Hulme refers to the theme is *vanitas vanitatum*, the despair and disillusion which Eliot considered to be "essential moments in the progress of the intellectual soul." The same theme predominates in his own early poetry. The mood is expressed both in images of desolation :

> "The worlds revolve like ancient women
>   Gathering fuel in vacant lots,"

and in the caustic satire of the Sweeney poems and the other four-line stanza poems of the 1920 volume. This, as Hulme says, is the starting point for the religious attitude. Disillusion, despair, scepticism, irreverence and blasphemy, are mental states possible only for a man who *cares* about existence ; they are perverse indications of the presence of a will to believe.

The main poem in the 1920 volume is *Gerontion*. The tone of bitter satire which predominates in the volume as a whole, is absent from this poem. It is the one which contains the seed of the poet's future development. By that I do not mean that is at all sanguine, but that in it we find for the first time unmistakably religious categories of thought. It is not at all clear who the person addressed as "you" in the following passage is intended to be, but the last line inclines me to think that God is meant rather than the reader of the poem.

> "I would meet you upon this honestly.
> I that was near your heart was removed therefrom
> To lose beauty in terror, terror in inquisition.
> I have lost my passion : why should I need to keep it
> Since what is kept must be adulterated?
> I have lost my sight, smell, hearing, taste and touch :
> How should I use them for your closer contact?"

The poem is a dramatic monologue, but I think that in these lines we hear the authentic voice of the poet. The feeling that "all is vanity" here reaches its extreme in the realisation of the vanity of the life of the senses. Such a realisation is a common stage in the development of the saint in all religions. It occasions the Christian's mortification of the flesh and the Buddhist's willed contemplation of the pure Mind-Essence. The last quoted line from Eliot's poem seems to indicate that his sense of the vanity of the sensuous life was now something more than mere disillusion, that it had its origin in the desire for the transcendent experience of union with God. The sentence from St. John of the Cross which is one of the epigraphs to *Sweeney Agonistes* emphasises the poet's preoccupation with this idea: "Hence the soul cannot be possessed of the divine union, until it has divested itself of the love of created beings."

But Eliot was still a long way away from the Christian Faith, and in the same volume as *Gerontion* there appeared his bitterest satirical attack on the Church in the poem *The Hippopotamus*. But his despair had by now run its natural course into a positive religious attitude. The sustained vision of the spiritual desolation of the modern world that went into *The Waste Land* could only have proceeded from the mind of a man who felt himself to be, in a way, not involved in the scene that he observed. The poet at this stage is open to the charge of 'intelligent eclecticism' which he later levelled against Irving Babbitt; for although allusions to Biblical and other Christian literature abound in *The Waste Land*, the way of salvation which is preferred at the end of the poem is taken from the Hindu *Upanishads*. The message of the Thunder is 'Datta, dayadhvam, damyata' (Give, sympathise, control). The virtues of self-surrender, sympathy and self-control are certainly not inconsistent with the Christian ethic, but the Christian virtue which is conspicuously absent here is: faith. Faith is irrational, and consequently for the intellectual soul it is the greatest obstacle to concurrence with Christian belief. By the time he completed *The Waste Land* Eliot had brought himself to the threshold of faith, but he was incapable of giving assent to the dogma without feeling that he would thereby do violence to his ideal of intellectual honesty.

T. E. Hulme undoubtedly influenced Eliot profoundly at some stage in his life. His *Speculations* were first published by Herbert Read in 1924. It is possible, however, that Eliot had access to the papers which made up this volume before they were published, or that he was personally acquainted with Hulme before the latter's death in the war in 1917. I don't want to appear to be tying my ends up too neatly, but it is certain that after 1924 a new note enters into Eliot's poetry, and it is at least possible that Hulme's book was partly responsible for it. Bearing in mind Eliot's situation at the time when *The Waste Land* was completed, consider the impression that the following passage from Hulme's *Humanism and the Religious Attitude* might have made on the poet :

> "What is important, is what nobody seems to realise—the dogmas like that of Original Sin, which are the closest expression of the categories of the religious attitude. That *man is in no sense perfect, but a wretched creature, who can yet apprehend perfection.* It is not, then, that I put up with the dogma for the sake of the sentiment, but that I may possibly swallow the sentiment for the sake of the dogma."[5] [Italics mine.]

It was essential that Eliot should realise the truth of the sentence I have italicised in the above paragraph, not as it applied to mankind generally, but as it applied to himself, before he became capable of the Christian humility which first makes its appearance in *Ash Wednesday* in the prayer : "Lord I am not worthy/but speak the word only."

It is in *The Hollow Men* (1925) that a recognisably Christian note is first struck. This poem is as expressive of disillusionment as any that has gone before. Indeed, what Mr. Wyndham Lewis has called its "drained-out cadences and desiccated vocables" evoke a sense of utter desolation.

The one hope of the hollow men is that the eyes may reappear, consciousness and a sense of purpose be restored to them. But there is always the Shadow interposed between them and reality, rendering them impotent and existence meaningless, and inexorably forcing them to acknowledge the Catholic dogma of supernatural Grace.

> "Between the idea
> And the reality
> Between the motion
> And the act
> Falls the Shadow
> > *For Thine is the Kingdom*
>
> Between the conception
> And the creation
> Between the emotion
> And the response
> Falls the Shadow
> > *Life is very long*."

The broken lines towards the end of the poem:

> "For Thine is
> Life is
> For Thine is the"

may be interpreted as an unsuccessful attempt to pray.

Ash Wednesday (1930) is the first of Eliot's poems which is wholly pervaded with Christian thought and feeling. As its title suggests, the poem is on the theme of purgation, purification and penitence. It is a wholly subjective and personal poem, and in this contrasts with *The Waste Land*. In it the main preoccupation of the poet is that of the saint and the mystic: to attain to union with God. The mood of the poem is so close to that of the early English mystical book, *The Cloud of Unknowing*, that a passage from the sixth chapter of that book provides considerable light for the critic to work by:

"He may well be loved, but not thought. By love may He be gotten and holden ; but by thought never. And therefore, although it be good sometime to think of the kindness and worthiness of God in special, and although it be a light and a part of contemplation : nevertheless yet in this work it shall be cast down and covered with a cloud of forgetting. And thou shalt step above it stalwartly, but listily, with a devout and a pleasing stirring of love, and try for to pierce that darkness above thee. And smite upon that thick cloud of unknowing with a sharp dart of longing love; and go not thence for thing that befalleth."[6]*

The first poem in the *Ash Wednesday* sequence opens on the old familiar note of *vanitas vanitatum*. It takes up the mood of the lines I have already quoted from *Gerontion*, but carries it further, for here it is not only the vanity of the sensuous life that is realised, but also that of the intellectual, rational life ("The infirm glory of the positive hour").

"Because I do not hope to turn again
Because I do not hope
Because I do not hope to turn
Desiring this man's gift and that man's scope
I no longer strive to strive towards such things

.   .   .   .   .

Because I do not hope to know again
The infirm glory of the positive hour

.   .   .   .   .

Because I cannot hope to turn again
Consequently I rejoice, having to construct something
Upon which to rejoice"

* Eliot was certainly acquainted with *The Cloud of Unknowing*, because a line from the last movement of *Little Gidding* ("With the drawing of this Love and the voice of this Calling") is taken direct from its second chapter. And it may not be wholly irrelevant to point out the similarity between the cloud of unknowing and the Shadow in *The Hollow Men*.

The willed effort to "construct something upon which to rejoice" had occupied Eliot during the years intervening between the composition of *The Hollow Men* and *Ash Wednesday*. It was during this period that he was finally converted to Anglo-Catholicism. But that act did not put an end to the struggles and debates of the intellectual soul. He had won through to faith, but God was still remote. As the anonymous author of *The Cloud of Unknowing* realised, the intellectual processes which had brought the poet so far would only be a hindrance to his attaining communion with God: "By love may He be gotten and holden; but by thought never." The poem therefore continues:

> "And pray to God to have mercy upon us
> And I pray that I may forget
> These matters that with myself I too much discuss
> Too much explain."

The intellectual power which he had formerly wielded is now as useless as the 'agèd eagle's' wings. He must learn to lose his own will in the will of God, to purge himself by waiting with infinite patience and without hope ("For hope would be hope for the wrong thing");

> "Because these wings are no longer wings to fly
> But merely vans to beat the air
> The air which is now thoroughly small and dry
> Smaller and drier than the will
> Teach us to care and not to care
> Teach us to sit still."

The third poem in the *Ash Wednesday* sequence tells in allegorical form of the soul's progress towards the unitive state. The progress is represented as the act of climbing a series of stairs. Here again the correspondence with the quoted passage from *The Cloud of Unknowing* is notable. In the latter book the reader is told stalwartly to step above the cloud of forgetting and to try to pierce the darkness of

the cloud of unknowing. In Eliot's poem "the devil of the
stairs" corresponds to the obstacle of the cloud of forgetting.
He wears "The deceitful face of hope and despair." Hope
and despair both have to be overcome; and several lines
later the poet has obtained "strength beyond hope and
despair/Climbing the third stair." Another obstacle is the
old one of the distracting life of the senses. Through a
slotted window there is revealed an enchanting landscape
and pastoral scene. The poet gives us a sensuous image:

> "Blown hair is sweet, brown hair over the mouth blown,
>   Lilac and brown hair;"

but he must pass beyond this distraction and continue his
journey up the stairs. But his own efforts, however strenuous,
will be vain without the aid of God's grace, and therefore the
poem ends with the prayer:

> "Lord, I am not worthy,
>   Lord, I am not worthy
>   but speak the word only."*

In his essay on Dante, Eliot says that "The souls in purgatory suffer because they *wish to suffer*, for purgation."
Purgation, and particularly purgation through suffering, is,
as I have said, the subject of *Ash Wednesday*; but it is a
subject which recurs constantly in Eliot's work. In *Murder
in the Cathedral*, Becket, immediately before the entrance of
the knights who are to kill him, says:

> "We have only to conquer
> Now, by suffering."

And in *The Family Reunion* Agatha says:

* These words are taken from Matthew viii. 8, where Jesus offers to go
and heal the Centurion's servant, and the Centurion answers: "Lord, I am
not worthy that thou shouldest come under my roof: but speak the word only
and my servant shall be healed." To the Catholic they have another significance, for these are words (with the substitution of 'soul' for 'servant') that
the priest repeats at Communion when he holds up the consecrated Host.

"To rest in our own suffering
Is evasion of suffering. We must learn to suffer more."

The same idea is behind much of the poetry of *Four Quartets*, and it is particularly explicit in the fourth movement of *East Coker*:

"The chill ascends from feet to knees,
The fever sings in mental wires.
If to be warmed, then I must freeze
And quake in frigid purgatorial fires
Of which the flame is roses, and the smoke is briars."

Again, in *Little Gidding*, we read:

"The only hope, or else despair
Lies in the choice of pyre or pyre—
To be redeemed from fire by fire."

This theme of purgation, which first appears in *Ash Wednesday*, became an integral part of Eliot's mature thought, bound up with his meditations on time, the Incarnation and the experience of transcendent vision in *Four Quartets*. It entered his work partly because it entered his life, and partly because he had come round to accepting the Christian view of man as "a wretched creature, who can yet apprehend perfection." If he could apprehend perfection he ought to raise himself towards that apprehension. And that he could only do through "prayer, observance, discipline, thought and action." Willed purgation was the necessary preliminary to the God-given moment of illuminative vision, of revelation. In *Ash Wednesday*, however, the poet does not experience such a revelation and the final poem in the sequence ends with the two lines:

"Suffer me not to be separated
And let my cry come unto Thee."

the first of which echoes Pascal's memorial: "Que je n'en jamais séparé," and the second of which carries us forward to *Four Quartets*.

Between *Ash Wednesday* and *Four Quartets* come the four *Ariel Poems*. These form a definite link between the two major works. In *Animula* the familiar theme of the struggles and debates of the intellectual soul and the conflict between instinct and consciousness is again stated:

> "The heavy burden of the growing soul
> Perplexes and offends more, day by day;
> Week by week, offends and perplexes more
> With the imperatives of 'is and seems'
> And may and may not, desire and control."

Marina, however, looks forward. It is the monologue of the aged king Pericles after his daughter had been lost at sea and then restored to him. The theme of the poem is resurrection. Both in imagery and subject matter it anticipates *Four Quartets*.

Four Quartets is Eliot's finest achievement, a work in which intellectual, religious and personal experience are welded together into a profound unity. The poet's success here in finding "the emotional equivalent of thought" makes the work inexhaustible in meaning but irreducible to the terms of discursive thought. As with most of Eliot's work, we feel that it was written not so much for the purpose of self-expression as for self-exploration. His starting point is the experience of certain brief moments of illuminative vision (such as those described by Martin Buber in the quotation on p. 148), and the desire to relate these to life as a whole. The process of generation of *Four Quartets* is described in the lines from *The Dry Salvages*:

> "We had the experience but missed the meaning
> And approach to the meaning restores the experience
> In a different form."

It was to approach to the meaning of those moments in human experience which are "in and out of time" that *Four*

Quartets was written. The poem is a sustained meditation, and in the passionate concentration of the meditation the experience was in a sense restored; so that the sensitive reader of the poem can himself experience the feeling of having transcended time.

Four Quartets is concerned with the eternal philosophical and religious questions about existence, particularly as they present themselves to the Christian mind: death and eternity, the purpose and conduct of life, the meaning of suffering and the redemption of sin, the nature of time and the significance of the Incarnation. In these four poems we have Eliot's mature thought, the "crown upon his lifetime's effort."

In the fourth poem in *Ash Wednesday* occur the words "Redeem the time." The redemption of time is the redemption of sin, the reversion of death, the consummation of life. How is it to be achieved? Paradoxicaliy, "Only through time time is conquered." Man's dual nature, at once finite and infinite, aspiring and held down, is a condition which must be accepted before it can be transcended. We can only reach "the still point of the turning world. . . . Where past and future are gathered" in transient moments; and these are moments when, to borrow a phrase from *The Rock*, "ecstasy is too much pain." The experience of pure being, of the moment when time is suspended, though it invests life with meaning, is too intense to be borne for long; and

> "the enchainment of past and future
> Woven in the weakness of the changing body
> Protects mankind from heaven and damnation
> Which flesh cannot endure."

Thus in *Burnt Norton* the paradoxical situation of man is stated. He is involved in the process of time. His normal daily life is conducted not in the eternal present moment, but with reference to time past and time future. That is what he means by living. But "that which is only living/Can only die." To the religious mind the idea that man is mortal is unacceptable. From its own experience it knows that there are moments which come within time, unpredictably, in the course of ordinary life, but which are themselves immortal and give man an intimation of quite another order of being. Of such a kind were

> "the moment in the rose-garden,
> The moment in the arbour where the rain beat,
> The moment in the draughty church at smokefall."

The problem is how to bring these experiences into life, thereby redeeming time and confounding death.

There are two ways. In *The Family Reunion* Agatha compares them :

"There are hours when there seems to be no past or future,
  Only a present moment of pointed light
  When you want to burn. When you stretch out your hand
  To the flames. They only come once,
  Thank God, that kind. Perhaps there is another kind,
  I believe, across a whole Thibet of broken stones
  That lie, fang up, a lifetime's march."

The first is the way of the visionary, the second that of the saint. The first is a shattering experience, for it takes us unawares (again, compare Pascal's memorial, p. 24); the second, the saint's apprehension of "The point of intersection of the timeless/With time," is

> "something given
> And taken, in a lifetime's death in love,
> Ardour and selflessness and self-surrender."

The majority of us cannot hope to emulate the saint, and consequently

> "For most of us, there is only the unattended
> Moment, the moment in and out of time,
> The distraction fit, lost in a shaft of sunlight,
> The wild thyme unseen, or the winter lightning
> Or the waterfall, or music heard so deeply
> That it is not heard at all, but you are the music
> While the music lasts."

But we must not depend on the chance occurrence of these moments. They are apprehensions of transcendence, and should therefore condition our living. We should try to follow them up by means of a milder form of the saint's asceticism :

> "These are only hints and guesses,
> Hints followed by guesses ; and the rest
> Is prayer, observance, discipline, thought and action."

Being human, however, we remain divided within, and

> "For most of us, this is the aim
> Never here to be realised ;
> Who are only undefeated
> Because we have gone on trying."

Life is real only when it is lived in the consciousness of death, and in the knowledge that death can be overcome. Eliot is as vehement as Rilke in deprecating the "unhealthy souls" who distract their minds from the fact of their mortality. In *The Rock* he says :

> "Life you may evade, but Death you shall not.
> You shall not deny the Stranger."

In *Murder in the Cathedral* he portrayed a man who did not evade death, but rather welcomed it, and indeed brought it upon himself. Becket had apprehended "The point of inter-section of the timeless/With time," and was therefore prepared for his martyrdom :

> "I have had a tremour of bliss, a wink of heaven, a whisper,
> And I would no longer be denied ; all things
> Proceed to a joyful consummation."

The process of purgation which he went through and which is symbolised by the dismissal of the four Tempters was an essential preliminary to his martyrdom :

> "All my life
> I have waited. Death will only come when I am worthy,
> And when I am worthy there is no danger.
> I have therefore only to make perfect my will."

The last line of this is echoed in the admonition of The Rock:

> "I say to you: *Make perfect your will.*
> I say: take no thought of the harvest,
> But only of the proper sowing."

The making perfect of the will is accomplished through "prayer, observance, discipline, thought and action." It is the act of preparing for death and for the overcoming of death, the way of bringing the timeless into the dimension of the temporal, of perpetuating and relating to ordinary life those moments of sharpened perception in which we experience our immortality.

For the Christian believer the paradox of time being transcended is not an impossibility, because it has actually happened. The Incarnation of the Son of God in Jesus of Nazareth is conceived as being the axis of history, the event which gave all subsequent time meaning and direction. In *The Rock* this central dogma of the Christian Faith is expounded:

> "Then came, at a predetermined moment, a moment in
>   time and of time,
> A moment not out of time, but in time, in what we
>   call history: transecting, bisecting the world of time, a
>   moment in time but not like a moment of time,
> A moment in time but time was made through that
>   moment: for without the meaning there is no time, and
>   that moment of time gave the meaning."

The Incarnation lies at the centre of Eliot's thought in *Four Quartets*. But it is his purpose to show that all those acts and all those moments in which time is transcended are, in a sense, incarnations; and that we are all able to redeem time and overcome sin and death in ourselves. It is significant that on the one occasion when the word is used it is not *The* Incarnation that is referred to, but simply Incarnation:

"The hint half guessed, the gift half understood, is Incarnation.
Here the impossible union
Of spheres of existence is actual,
Here past and future
Are conquered, and reconciled."

Incarnation, then, is to be taken in a general sense to mean the intersection of the timeless moment with time. In the Christian scriptures there are other instances of this having happened, and two of them are important themes in the poem: the Annunciation in *The Dry Salvages*, and the Pentecost in *Little Gidding*.

It is not my purpose here to write an exegesis of *Four Quartets*. The above brief explanation of what I believe to be the central thought structure of the poem should be sufficient to relate it to the earlier work, to suggest the scope and nature of the poet's mature thought, and to show that it is by means of such thought that the intellectual soul arrives at faith.

III

"The isolation that prevails everywhere, above all in our age—it has not fully developed, it has not reached its limit yet. For everyone strives to keep his individuality as apart as possible, wishes to secure the greatest possible fullness of life for himself; but meantime all his efforts result not in attaining fullness of life but self-destruction, for instead of self-realisation he ends by arriving at complete solitude. All mankind in our age have split up into units, they all keep apart, each in his own groove; each one holds aloof, hides himself and hides what he has, from the rest, and he ends by being repelled by others and repelling them. He heaps up riches by himself and thinks, 'how strong I am now and how secure', and in his madness he does not understand that the more he heaps up, the more he sinks into self-destructive impotence. For he is accustomed to rely upon himself alone and to cut himself off from the whole ; he has trained himself not to believe in the help of others, in men and in humanity, and only trembles for fear he should lose his money and the privileges that he has won for himself. Everywhere in these days men have, in their mockery, ceased to understand that the true security is to be found in social solidarity rather than in isolated individual effort. But his terrible individualism must inevitably have an end, and all will suddenly understand how unnaturally they are separated from one another. It will be the spirit of the time, and people will marvel that they have sat so long in darkness without seeing the light. And then the sign of the Son of Man will be seen in the heavens. . . . But, until then, we must keep the banner flying. Sometimes even if he has to do it alone, and his conduct seems to be crazy, a man must set an example, and so draw men's souls out of their solitude, and spur them to some act of brotherly love, that the great idea may not die."[7]

This paragraph from the teaching of the dying Russian monk, Father Zossima, in Dostoevsky's *The Brothers Karamazov*, summarises the situation which has confronted the modern poets we have considered, or rather the situation in which they have been involved. For, with the exception of Eliot, all our poets have been adamant individualists, in opposition against the established Church, and for the most part concurring with Thomas's view that Christianity is a "spent lie". It is true that "the great poet, in writing himself, writes his time", but both the selves and the time which these poets have documented have been chaotic, and, though they may have found their personal solutions to their predicament, these have invariably been invalid in the wider world. Eliot alone would have agreed with Father Zossima that "the true security is to be found in social solidarity rather than in isolated individual effort." His

> Descend lower, descend only
> Into the world of perpetual solitude

was but an interim solution to the modern poet's dilemma; whereas for most of the other poets it was the solution which they finally adopted.

Eliot is the most socially conscious and the most moral of the poets we have studied. If asked in what sense moral? I would reply, in the sense in which Bradley uses the term in the second essay in his *Ethical Studies*. Here, again, one of the central problems with which this book has been concerned is touched upon. What I have called the emergence from chaos, Bradley speaks of as an achievement of 'homogeneity'; and he equates 'homogeneity' and 'self-realisation', defining the latter as the realisation of oneself, not as an individual, but as a constituent part of a social whole. Someone has remarked on the influence of Bradley on Eliot's prose style. I would suggest that the influence goes much deeper. And whether it does or not, Eliot would certainly endorse Bradley's ideas as expressed in the following passage:

> "I am to be perfectly homogeneous; but that I cannot be unless fully specified, and the question is, How can I be extended so as to take in my external relations? Goethe has said, 'be a whole *or* join a whole', but to that we must answer, 'You cannot be a whole, *unless* you join a whole.'"[8]

Bradley is aware of the stumbling block which arises in the way of the imaginative, creative man in the shape of the fact that the interests of the whole and those of the individual who is a part, often conflict with each other. Thus society's "more" means my "less", and "the greater specification of the whole means the making me more special, more narrowed and limited, and less developed within myself." This "greater specification of the whole" is what Kierkegaard called the "levelling process", and most of our poets have sought refuge from it in Kierkegaardian subjectivity. They have chosen to *be* a whole. Bradley and Eliot maintain that this is not possible. The achievement of Rilke, Rimbaud and others would seem to indicate that it is. How can we resolve this crucial question?

The question can be put in a more manageable form if we ask what is meant by the term 'self-realisation'. Bradley believes, as we have seen, that the term is only applicable to the action of a person who realises himself as a member of a community. Eliot, believing that "men cannot get on without giving allegiance to something outside themselves", would corroborate this idea. In Kierkegaard, on the other hand, self-realisation is an entirely subjective matter. The great poets of our time have tended on the whole, to line up with Kierkegaard. This is probably because, as poets, they have been concerned primarily with maintaining their creative faculties in working order, and only secondarily with pre-serving a cultural tradition or furthering civilisation. While admitting the importance of man's external, social relations, I do not see how we can say, as Bradley presumably would have done, that poets like Rilke, Rimbaud and Yeats failed to attain self-realisation. Certainly they did it to a different degree and in a different way from Eliot, but unfortunately self-realisation is such an ill-defined concept in western thought that we have no terms to distinguish the degrees or stages in the process. The Buddhist distinguishes at least five stages, and can trace the different degrees of self-realisation from the disciple to the master, the Arhat, the Bodhisattva and finally the Tathagata. He does not, how-ever, make the distinction with which we are concerned here, and which is typically western, between purely subjective self-realisation and realisation of oneself as a member of a community. Very few of those people who are endowed with an exceptional degree of consciousness, succeed in resolving the conflict between these two, and in identifying their own particular will with the will of the whole. Eliot is one of the few who have done so in our time. If this is creditable (and it is certainly one very satisfactory way out of the predicament in which the modern man finds himself), it must be remembered that Eliot was constitutionally and intellectually predisposed to the act of commitment, which would have been impossible for Thomas, Whitman, Yeats, Rimbaud or Rilke.

This raises the question whether we can judge one poet greater than another just by reason of his psychology. Considering him purely as a poet, of course, we can't. But it will have been clear throughout this book that my critical criteria have been religious and ethical rather than literary. My ideal has been the fully conscious modern man, the man who has seen the darker side of life, howled in the abyss, but managed to emerge a yea-sayer ; and who has, after experiencing profound inner division, succeeded in reintegrating himself on a higher level. It may be argued that both Rilke and Eliot, even Rimbaud, succeeded in doing this, and that my choice of Eliot as the subject of this last chapter is arbitrary and dictated by personal predilection. I would not deny this latter point. When reading Eliot I find myself in a familiar intellectual climate, a tradition which I can understand and of which I feel myself to be a part. His declaration that "If Christianity goes, the whole of our culture goes" demands to be weighed and considered carefully. Yet I cannot advocate that we should all become Catholics and adopt *The Idea of a Christian Society* as our new Social Contract. Nor can I dismiss such a poet as Rilke as a "heretic", for I am not convinced that the way of the intellectual soul is intrinsically better than that of the visionary individualist. What I do believe—and this is why I have made Eliot the subject of this final chapter—is that the way of the intellectual soul, because it requires no suspension of consciousness, but is followed when our normal senses and intellectual operations are at their highest pitch of discipline, is the way to religious truth which those of us who are not mystics can most easily understand and most profitably follow.

The solution to the problem of self-realisation lies some-where between the ideas expressed by Father Zossima in the passage quoted at the beginning of this section, and those of Jung in the following extract from *Psychotherapy Today* :

"If man cannot exist without society, neither can he exist without oxygen, water, albumen, fat and so on. Like these, society is one of the necessary conditions for his existence. It would be ludicrous to maintain that man exists in order to breathe air. It is equally ludicrous to say that man exists for the sake of society. 'Society' is nothing more than the concept of the symbiosis of a group of human beings. A concept is not a carrier of life. The sole and natural carrier of life is the individual, and this holds true throughout nature."[9]

There is a profound truth both in Father Zossima's and in Jung's statement. The problem of the poet in our time is to reconcile the two. Father Zossima criticised the "terrible individualism" of modern man, whereas Jung asserts that the sole carrier of life, the agent of progress in civilization, is the individual. For a poet like Eliot, however, there is no contradiction there. He would agree that the individual is the carrier of life, but would insist that he can only be such when he works within a living tradition. He would acknow-ledge that the artist is often by nature a nonconformist and confirmed individualist, but would say that if he is a great artist he will feel the need to extinguish his own mere private personality and merge himself into a larger whole. He will also have the historical sense, the sense "not only of the pastness of the past, but of the presence" ; and will thus feel responsible for the future. And he will therefore be com-pelled to agree with Eliot that "Our problem being to form the future, we can only form it on the materials of the past ; we must *use* our heredity, instead of denying it." He will be led inexorably to assent to the dogmas of the Christian Faith.

It may be argued, though, that there is a sense in which Rilke is closer to the spirit of Christianity, to the teachings and sensibility of its founder, than Eliot. So, perhaps, was Dostoevsky, and the "great idea" that Father Zossima wished to preserve may be a very different thing from the Faith which Eliot believes will "renew and rebuild civilization, and save the World from suicide." The poets and thinkers of the immediate future have the same world to live in, the same problems to confront, the same chaos to transcend, within themselves and without, as the poets with whom this book has been concerned. We are only better off than they because we inherit their experience. But we have to find our own truth, and even if we cannot accept Eliot's solution, his teaching is one of the things we must not lose sight of in our search.

NOTES

PART ONE

Chapter One

Page 17. 1. Leonardo da Vinci: *Selections from the Notebooks* (ed. Irma Richter; World's Classics, Oxford University Press, 1952), p. 281.

Page 19. 2. R. W. Emerson: *The Over-Soul. Essays.* (Everyman Edition, 1906), p. 150.

3. Scholem, Gershom: *Major Trends in Jewish Mysticism* (Thames & Hudson, 1955), p. 7.

Page 20. 4. Blake, William: *Jerusalem* (*Poetry and Prose*, Nonesuch Centenary Edition), p. 436.

Page 21. 5. Berkeley, George: *A New Theory Of Vision and Other Writings* (Everyman Library, 1910), p. 126.

Page 23. 6. Quoted by William James in *The Varieties of Religious Experience* (Longmans, Green, 1919), p. 80.

Chapter Two

Page 30. 1. *Theologia Germanica* (tr. Susanna Winkworth; Gollancz 1951), p. 127.

Page 31. 2. Dostoevsky, Fyodor: *The Brothers Karamazov* (tr. Constance Garnett; Heinemann, 1951), p. 250.

3. *A Treasury of Russian Literature* (ed. B. G. Guerney; The Bodley Head, 1948), pp. 459-460.

Page 37. 4. Jung, C. G.: *Psychological Reflections* (ed. Jacobi; Routledge & Kegan Paul, 1953), p. 29.

Page 38. 5. Quoted by Evelyn Underhill in *Mysticism* (Methuen, 1930), p. 86, from Récéjac's *Essay on the Bases of the Mystic Knowledge*, tr. S. C. Upton.

Page 41. 6. Hulme, T. E.: *Speculations* (Kegan Paul, 1924), p. 147.

Chapter Three

Page 46. 1. cf. Hulme, T. E.: *Speculations* (ed. cit.), p. 47. The whole of this chapter was profoundly influenced by Hulme's essay *Humanism and the Religious Attitude*.

Page 47. 2. Shaw, G. B.: *Prefaces* (Odhams, 1938), p. 542.

Page 49. 3. Yeats, W. B.: *Collected Poems* (Macmillan, 1952), p. 167.

Page 51. 4. Yeats, W. B.: *Essays* (Macmillan, 1924), p. 440.

Page 52. 5. Quoted by Evelyn Underhill in *Mysticism* (Methuen, 1930), p. 37, from *De Vera Contemplatione*, chap. 12.

Page 52.   6. Quoted by Joseph Bernhart in his Notes to the *Theologia Germanica* (Gollancz, 1951), p. 238.

7. Nietzsche, F. W.: *Thus Spake Zarathustra* (tr. A. Tille and M. M. Bozman, Everyman Edition, 1950), p. 77.

Page 55.   8. Eliot, T. S.: *The Pensées of Pascal* (in *Selected Essays*; Faber & Faber, 1951; p. 408).

9. Dostoevsky, Fyodor: *The Brothers Karamazov* (tr. Constance Garnett; Heinemann, 1951), p. 241.

Page 58.   10. Malraux, André: *Essays on the Psychology of Art*, Vol. 1, *Museum Without Walls* (tr. Stuart Gilbert; A. Zwemmer, 1949), pp. 128-129.

Chapter Four

Page 59.   1. Quoted by F. H. Heinemann in *Existentialism and the Modern Predicament* (A. & C. Black, 1953), p. 35.

Page 60.   2. Eliot, T. S.: *The Waste Land* (in *Collected Poems*; Faber & Faber, 1936; p. 77).

Page 61.   3. Yeats, W. B.: *Autobiographies* (Macmillan, 1955), p. 192.

Page 63.   4. Marcel, Gabriel: *Men Against Humanity* (tr. G. S. Fraser; Harvill Press, 1952), p. 193.

5. Quoted by Victor Gollancz in *A Year of Grace*, p. 135, from C. de B. Evans' translation (Watkins).

Page 65.   6. Used by Yeats as the epigraph to his poem, *Politics*.

Page 66.   7. Hulme, T. E.: *Speculations* (ed. cit.), p. 55.

Page 67.   8. Baudelaire, Charles: *Intimate Journals* (tr. Isherwood, Methuen, 1949), p. 20.

9. Jung, C. G.: *Psychological Reflections* (ed. cit.), p. 305.

10. Wells, H. G.: *The Open Conspiracy and Other Writings* (London, 1933), p. 27.

Page 68.   11. Jeans, Sir James: *The Growth of Physical Science* (Cambridge University Press, 1950), p. 328.

Page 69.   12. Ibid., p. 294.

13. This maxim is, I understand, inscribed on a wall in Princeton University. I am not sure of its source in Einstein's writings.

Page 71.   14. Heinemann, F. H.: *Existentialism and the Modern Predicament* (ed. cit.), p. 9.

15. Jeans, Sir James: *The Growth of Physical Science* (ed. cit.), p. 294.

16. Hulme, T. E.: *Speculations* (ed. cit.), p. 228.

17. Quoted by F. H. Heinemann in *Existentialism and the Modern Predicament* (ed. cit.), p. 112.

Page 72.   18. Ibid., p. 52.

19. Ibid., p. 99.

Page 73.   20. Ibid., p. 114.

PART TWO

*Works sited from the authors given special consideration in the
following chapters are listed in "Acknowledgments" on page 5.*

Chapter One

Page 77.   1. Spender, Stephen: *June 1940* (in *Collected Poems*; Faber & Faber, 1955; p. 132).

Page 82.   2. Boehme, Jacob: *Of the Supersensual Life* (Everyman Edition of *The Signature of All Things*, etc., p. 230).

Page 88.   3. Traherne, Thomas: *Centuries of Meditations* (Dobell, 1927), p. 151.

Chapter Two

Page 95.   1. Kierkegaard, Søren: *Concluding Unscientific Postscript* (tr. David F. Swenson & Walter Lowrie; Oxford University Press, 1941), p. 113.
2. James, Henry: *Mr. Walt Whitman* (in *The Portable Henry James*; Viking Press, New York, 1951; p. 432).
3. Ibid., p. 489.

Chapter Three

Page 113.   1. Jaspers, Karl; *Man in the Modern Age* (tr. E. & C. Paul; Routledge & Kegan Paul, 1951), p. 146.

Page 131.   2. *Isaiah* 6, vi-vii.

Chapter Four

Page 138.   1. *Theologia Germanica* (tr. Susanna Winkworth; Gollancz, 1951), p. 134.

Page 139.   2. Baudelaire, Charles: *Intimate Journals* (ed. cit.), p. 30.

Page 141.   3. The translations from *Une Saison en Enfer* quoted in this chapter are by Norman Cameron (*A Season in Hell*, John Lehmann, 1949).

Page 142.   4. Quoted by Wallace Fowlie in his book, *Rimbaud's Illuminations* (Harvill Press, 1953), p. 143.
5. Quotations from the *Illuminations* throughout this chapter are in the translation by Wallace Fowlie (ed. cit.).

Page 148.   6. Buber, Martin: *I and Thou* (tr. Ronald Gregor Smith; T. & T. Clark, 1937), p. 31.

Page 152.   7. Translation by Norman Cameron: *Selected Verse Poems of Arthur Rimbaud* (Hogarth Press, 1942), p. 41.

Page 156.   8. Ibid., p. 17.

Page 157.   9. Translation by Ben Belitt: *Four Poems by Rimbaud: the Problem of Translation* (Sylvan Press, 1948).

Chapter Five

Page 166.   1. Quoted by Erich Heller in *The Disinherited Mind* (Bowes & Bowes, 1952), p. 127.

Page 169.   2. *Thomas Mann's Stories and Episodes* (Everyman, 1940), p. 33.

Page 170.   3. Quotations from Rilke's letters throughout this chapter are in the translation by R. F. C. Hull (*Selected Letters of Rainer Maria Rilke*; Macmillan, 1947).
4. Quoted by J. B. Leishman in his Introduction to *Requiem and Other Poems*. I have used Mr. Leishman's excellent translations of Rilke's poems throughout this chapter where possible. The books in which they occur are as follows: *Requiem and Other Poems* (Hogarth Press, 1949); *Sonnets to Orpheus* (Hogarth Press, 1949); and *Duino Elegies* (tr. J. B. Leishman & Stephen Spender; Hogarth Press, 1952).

Page 171.   5. Translations of poems from *Das Stundenbuch* are by Babette Deutsch (*Poems from the Book of Hours*; Vision Press, 1947).

Page 175.   6. Passages from *The Notebook of Malte Laurids Brigge* are translated by John Linton (Hogarth Press, 1950).

Page 177.   7. The complete text of *Erlebnis* is printed in Appendix III of Leishman & Spender's translation of the *Duino Elegies*.

Page 181.   8. Nietzsche, F. W.: *Thus Spake Zarathustra* (ed. cit.), p. 184.

Page 182.   9. Fragment 57 (Bywater). *Early Greek Philosophy* by John Burnet (A. & C. Black, 1930), p. 137.

Page 186.   10. Berdyaev, Nicolas: *Spirit and Reality* (tr. George Reavey; Geoffrey Bles, 1946), p. 64.

Chapter Six

Page 191.   1. Whitehead, A. N.: *Religion in the Making*. In *Alfred North Whitehead, An Anthology* (Selected by F. S. C. Northrop & M. W. Gross; Cambridge University Press, 1953), p. 513.

Page 192.   2. *Selected Essays* (Faber & Faber, 1951), p. 387. All prose passages in this chapter, except where otherwise stated, are taken from this edition of the *Selected Essays*.

Page 193.   3. In *The Poetry Review*, July & October, 1955.

Page 198.   4. Hulme, T. E.: *Speculations* (ed. cit.), p. 22.

Page 200.   5. Ibid., p. 71.

Page 202.   6. *The Cloud of Unknowing* (John M. Watkins, 1934), pp. 77-78.

Page 212.   7. Dostoevsky, Fyodor: *The Brothers Karamazov* (ed. cit.), pp. 314-315.

Page 213.   8. Bradley, F. H.: *Ethical Studies* (Oxford University Press, 1927), p. 79.

Page 216.   9. Jung, C. G.: *Psychological Reflections* (ed. cit.), p. 152.